S

ESSAYS IN THE THEORY
OF ECONOMIC GROWTH

ESSAYS IN THE THEORY OF ECONOMIC GROWTH

JOAN ROBINSON

Time is a device to prevent everything
from happening at once.

BERGSON

MACMILLAN
London · Melbourne · Toronto
ST MARTIN'S PRESS
New York
1968

MACMILLAN AND CO LTD
Little Essex Street London WC2
and also at Bombay Calcutta and Madras
Macmillan South Africa (Publishers) Pty Ltd Johannesburg
The Macmillan Company of Australia Pty Ltd Melbourne
The Macmillan Company of Canada Ltd Toronto
St Martin's Press Inc New York

Printed in Great Britain by
Lowe & Brydone (Printers) Ltd., London

PREFACE

THE essays in this volume might be regarded as an introduction rather than as a supplement to my *Accumulation of Capital*. That book was found excessively difficult. The main fault, I think, lay in too terse an exposition of the main ideas, particularly in Chapter 8, and a failure to mark sufficiently sharply the departure from the confused but weighty corpus of traditional teaching that we are required to make when we adopt a Keynesian approach to long-period problems. I offer the present volume with apologies to readers whose heads ached over the earlier one.

In my experience a great deal of misunderstanding and argument at cross-purposes is caused by conflating notions derived from the Walrasian system of supply-and-demand prices with those derived from the Marshallian (or Marxian) conception of normal profits. The first essay endeavours to disentangle them.

The second, with its appendix, outlines a generalisation of the *General Theory* which I hope will be more perspicuous than my former attempts.

The most percipient of the critics of my *Accumulation* reproached me for a selective lowering of the degree of abstraction. Certainly it is not legitimate to set up a highly abstract model and then draw from it conclusions applicable to actual problems. In that book I dropped out here and there hints as to whither, in my own opinion, the analysis might be found to lead. This time I have refrained even from hints. My main concern is to get economic analysis off the mud of static equilibrium theory. Once it is afloat enticing voyages beckon in many directions.

The Model of Technical Progress makes the argument even more formalistic than the earlier version, but in doing so, I hope, clears up some points.

The Neo-neoclassical Theorem distils the essence of the analysis of the technical frontier which I made very heavy weather over at the first attempt.

Of outright errors in the *Accumulation* I have found two. The first was pointed out by Mr. Little and corrected in the reprint of the book. It concerned the point about Mr. Harrod's formula, now, I hope, correctly stated in the footnote on page 12. The second concerns the idea that when non-employment emerges as a result of growth in the labour force ahead of the demand for labour provided by the stock of capital equipment in existence, a fall in money wages may increase the rate of accumulation. The assumption is that (with unchanged profit expectations) gross investment has inertia in money terms so that a fall in the money wage rate increases net investment in real terms. This seems plausible enough, but it was wrong to conclude that the rate of accumulation could be stepped up by this means. After a once-for-all fall of money costs, amortisation quotas in money terms are adjusted and the inertia of gross investment would thereafter apply at the new, lower, level. On both these points I fell into error through failure to see the implications of my own basic ideas. The corrections make my analysis more so, not less so.

I am indebted to the editors of the *Quarterly Journal of Economics*, *Rivista di Politica Economica* and the *Review of Economic Studies*, for permission to reprint, respectively, the first, the third and part of the last of the following essays.

JOAN ROBINSON

CAMBRIDGE, *March* 1962

CONTENTS

Contents

ix

ESSAYS IN THE THEORY
OF ECONOMIC GROWTH

I

NORMAL PRICES

THE traditional teaching that goes under the title of the theory of Value and Distribution does not depict a single system of prices ; it consists of a variety of systems, each appropriate to the model of a different kind of economy.

The models can be divided into two broad classes, with a variety of intermediate types combining elements of each. In one class the main emphasis is on a vertical division between groups of producers with different endowments of factors suited (by quality or by the proportions in which they exist) to the production of different commodities. In the other, the emphasis is upon a horizontal division between the classes of society.

The problem is discussed in this essay in terms of a closed system with no economic activity of public authorities.

SUPPLY AND DEMAND

Prices imply exchange and exchange implies specialisation. In the first type of model the basis of specialisation lies in technical characteristics of factors of production. 'In the original state of society the labourer had neither landlord nor master to share with him.'[1] There was no price of labour ; the return to work was the physical product, to be consumed or traded. Adam Smith declared that in this situation 'the proportion between the quantities of labour necessary for acquiring different objects, seems to be the only circumstance which can afford any rule for exchanging them for one another'.[2] But where there are differences in the *quality* of labour this rule is of no use. If the hunters who traded beaver for deer belonged to different tribes, one settled on the river and the other on the hills, their trade would have been regulated by traditional rules,

[1] *Wealth of Nations* (Everyman's Library), i, 57.   [2] *Ibid.* p. 42.

or by the laws of supply and demand.

The basis of specialisation may lie in property in natural factors of production or in human skill and knowledge. In the model which serves for the so-called theory of international trade the factors exist in separate bundles of arbitrary composition. The same model can be made to serve for an economy in which workers with heritable skill and lore for various occupations own the means of production that they operate and exchange their outputs for each other.

To set this model up in its pure form we suppose that there is no employment of wage labour. The exchange of products is conceived to take place according to purely commercial principles (though in reality such trade is largely governed by traditional and ceremonial rules); each group of producers of a homogeneous commodity is sufficiently numerous for competition to prevail within it, in the sense that prices are independent of the volume of transactions of any one trader, and there is no collusion amongst them.

The conditions of supply and demand for tradeable commodities depend on the tastes and habits of the individuals concerned and the distribution of purchasing power between them; and on the prevailing techniques of production, the numbers of producers with different aptitudes, the natural resources available to them and the stock of produced means of production in existence (looms and stocks of yarn, spindles and stocks of flax, for the production of cloth; forges and stocks of iron, furnaces and stocks of ore, for the production of horseshoes; and so forth).

Any one set of conditions is satisfied by a particular pattern of outputs and prices. This is exhibited in the Walrasian general equilibrium system, and there is no need to rehearse it here.

The fact that equilibrium prices are ruling at a moment of time does not entail a stationary position. The equilibrium of supplies and demands may be such that investment is going on. Some demands, that is to say, may be for additions to stock. A blacksmith with two sons may be spending part of his current output of horseshoes upon having a forge built. A blacksmith with one son may consider that the advantage of the higher future output of horseshoes per unit of effort which would be provided by a more labour-saving forge is worth a present sacrifice of current consumables.

Moreover (a point that is not often stressed), there is no presumption that the equilibrium prices are such that everyone in the story can make a living. We start off with an arbitrary set of conditions, an arbitrary quantity of factors of production of each type and an arbitrary number of owners of factors. The prices that rule in equilibrium, at a particular moment, may well be such that some of the individuals in question are in process of being starved out of existence.

Interest, Lending and Saving

One of the problems that give rise to confusion is the nature of the monetary system that is being assumed. This model can be set up in a non-monetary form, in the sense that it contains no generally accepted unit of account or vehicle for storing purchasing power. Each family provides its own labour force. Each type of work brings its own return in kind. There is an equilibrium pattern of prices of commodities in terms of each other, but there is no general price level. For convenience, the observing economist may make his calculations in terms of units of one commodity chosen as a *numéraire*, but each family within the economy is interested in the purchasing power of its own products over whatever other things it would like to buy. The price level in terms of the *numéraire* is only the inverse of the purchasing power of a unit of one particular commodity, and it has no more significance than any other.

The fact that the model is non-monetary does not exclude lending at interest, so long as transactions are directly between the parties concerned ; there is no rediscounting and no market in second-hand debts (transferable obligations are the essence of money). Loans consist of a supply of commodities, to be consumed, used, or traded for others to be used or consumed, against a promise of future repayment. At any moment loans are offered by families whose receipts from production and trade (and from interest payments on past loans) have exceeded, over the recent past, their purchases of commodities to be consumed or added to their own stock of means of production ; that is to say, by families whose saving exceeds their own investment.

3

The supply of loanable funds is also fed by repayments of past loans which the creditor wishes to lend again. The demand for loans comes from families whose purchases for consumption and additions to stocks of means of production exceed their current receipts. The rate of interest at which loans are negotiated fluctuates from day to day under the varying pressures of supply and demand. (Since there is no riskless and costless store of value available to would-be lenders who desire to carry purchasing power forward, the rate of interest will be negative when there is a sufficiently strong pressure of supply relative to demand for loanable funds.)

For each individual family there is an expected marginal efficiency of investment in terms of its own products (for a blacksmith, the ratio of a flow of future horseshoes to the present horseshoe price of a forge) depending upon technical conditions and the relation between the labour available in the family and its existing stocks of means of production. Its subjective value to the family depends upon expectations about the future purchasing power of its products over various other commodities, and expectations about the future needs of the family. The influences governing its investment decisions are evidently extremely complex, but it is possible to say, in general, that a low rate of interest will tend to encourage both investment and consumption, for when the charge on a loan in terms of its own product is expected to be less than the marginal yield of the investment that it pays for, expected future income can be increased without the family itself having to provide any saving.[1]

Every change in the stock of means of production brings a new equilibrium pattern of prices into being. Conditions may be such that there are sharp corners for a particular commodity at which a small increase of output saturates requirements and brings its purchasing power down to starvation levels ; or a relative increase in output of other things sends its price shooting up ; one equilibrium position is then violently different from another, although containing only small differences in factor supplies.

[1] From the above account of the rate of interest in a non-monetary model it is possible to pick up the thread of several lines of thought which become sadly tangled when they are followed without further consideration into the problems of a modern industrial economy.

4

Normal Prices

A Static State

A stationary state obtains when the labour force is constant for each group of producers separately ; and when all families are satisfied with the stocks of means of production that they own, and are keeping them intact, so that gross investment is equal to wear and tear, item by item, and net saving is zero. With unchanging habits and tastes, there is an equilibrium pattern of outputs and prices corresponding to the supplies of all factors of production then in existence.

Individual families save so long as the return that they can get, on further investment in means of production for themselves or as interest on loans to others, exceeds their subjective preference for present over future consumption. Zero saving entails that the marginal efficiency of investment is equal, for all families, to the rate of discount which expresses that preference for the family for which it is lowest. Then, and only then, is there a uniform marginal productivity of investment throughout the economy.

The amount of outstanding debt is rather a matter of historical accident. Families who happen to be operating means of production that were not acquired by their own saving are paying interest to those who own wealth (the fruit of past saving) that happens to be in excess of the means of production which they operate. The rate of interest that is being paid on old debts must be only a little less than the marginal efficiency of investment, for an offer of loans at an appreciably lower rate would set investment going. (An offer at a higher rate would find no takers.)

It is to be observed that, even when these rigorous conditions are satisfied, there is nothing in the picture that corresponds to a *rate of profit on capital*. We can, if we like, value all the goods in existence at their equilibrium prices in terms of some *numéraire*, and call the resulting sum 'capital' ; and we can value the total net flow of production in the same terms, but there is no way of telling what part of that flow belongs to the 'capital' and what part to the work being done with the aid of the means of production which it comprises.[1]

---

[1] We can elaborate the model by allowing the artisans to employ workers — the unwanted younger sons or bastards of other families. Then, given the

The Meaning of Equilibrium

The general equilibrium analysis can do no more than depict the position corresponding to any one set of conditions, and compare the positions corresponding to specified differences in conditions. It can say nothing about the effects of changes in conditions.

An equilibrium position is stable, in a purely formal sense, when the relevant curves cut each other the right way. It is stable in a real-life sense, *once it has been reached*, when minor chance departures from it quickly reverse themselves.

It is quite another matter to say that it has the property of persisting through time. This would be true of the stationary state, provided that no change in basic conditions occurs and perfect tranquillity prevails. But an equilibrium position which contains accumulation of means of production, consumption of exhaustible resources or starvation for some group of producers, is in course of upsetting itself from within, and chance events may upset it from without. When an economy more or less corresponding to this model is in trading relations with a different type of economy, changes taking place in the latter may be drastically disturbing to it.

The time taken to get close to equilibrium from an arbitrary initial starting-point may be long, in some circumstances indefinitely long. (Walras guarded himself by supposing that the equilibrium position is discovered before any trade takes place.) Thus, when changes in the conditions are liable to occur, the analysis predicts that equilibrium is not likely ever to be realised.

To make the argument applicable to actual situations, we have to leave equilibrium analysis behind and approach the

amount of land and equipment that he owns, there is a definite marginal net product of labour to each employer, from which we can derive his demand curve for workers in terms of his own product. The level of wages, for raw hands, must be more or less the same in terms of whatever product it is earned. The marginal prospective return on investment in equipment then tends to be higher for everyone the easier the labour market : that is, the lower the cost of additional labour in terms of own product for each investor. Even so, there is no way of calculating the average return on equipment independently of the 'reward of enterprise' that the employer enjoys. When the number of employers going in for different lines of production varies with the prospective profits to be made in each, the model dissolves, for there are then no given supplies of specific factors.

problem in terms of an historical process, the system continually lurching from one out-of-equilibrium position to another.[1]

WAGES AND PROFITS

In the second type of model there are no persistent differences between factors of production. Labour can be trained and equipment designed for any use. To keep the argument simple we will postulate that all workers are alike.[2] Workers own no property and must take service with those who can provide means of production for them to operate.

An economy in which owners of property hire workers (directly or through the agency of managers of firms) cannot be conceived to operate without money, in the sense of some generally acceptable medium of exchange. Wage rates are agreed in terms of money and prices of products are established in terms of money. The real earnings of a worker and the real cost of labour to an employer then emerge from the relations between prices and wages in terms of money. Wage rates in terms of money are purely arbitrary. *Changes* in money-wage rates have important 'real' consequences, but *differences*, in equilibrium positions, affect nothing but the words and numbers used to describe prices and incomes and the number of units making up the stock of the medium of exchange. In what follows, all values are to be understood as relative to the level of money-wage rates.

Normal Prices

A firm (that is, the unit in which employment is organised) is not confined to any particular range of production, but can set

[1] The doctrine that market forces tend to establish equilibrium amongst traders in primary products, which is used to support opposition to any form of regulation in such markets, seems to be based upon a very superficial reading of the general equilibrium analysis.

[2] This is not necessary to the argument, provided that the supply of labour with different sorts of skills responds to differences in expected earnings in such a way that the return on an investment in training is everywhere the same. But when a worker's family provides for his training, it is artificial to regard his earnings as a return on investment ; and, if we did so, we should have to allow a different rate of profit on this type of investment from that expected on capitalist investment. Highly qualified employees are introduced in the third model.

7

labour to work upon whatever promises the best return. The choice amongst investment opportunities is therefore conceived to be made in such a way as to maximise the prospective profit on the sum of money committed. In this model competitive conditions have a different meaning from that required for the first model. There competition was a feature of the day-to-day operation of markets ; here it is a feature of long-run investment plans. Here it is not necessary that there should be a perfectly elastic demand for the output of each seller in each market at each moment of time ; it is necessary that there should be no limitation on access, given time, to any market, so that an equal rate of expected profit on investment tends to be established throughout the system. In a state of tranquillity, when expectations are realised, the criterion that competitive conditions prevail, in this sense, is that there is a uniform rate of net profit on the value of capital in all lines of production. The prices that obtain in these conditions are the 'normal long-run supply prices' of Marshall, or 'prices of production' of Marx.

The rate of profit on investment dominates the rate of interest on loans. True, when there is a market in second-hand debts (a stock exchange) the level of the rate of interest at which new loans are negotiated is strongly influenced by the prices obtaining in that market, and this, in turn, is strongly influenced by expectations about what the future level of the rate will be. Keynes' liquidity preference theory is designed to answer the questions : Why does anyone hold money (above the requirement for convenience balances) when it is possible to get interest on loans ? And the answer runs in terms of the relation between current and expected future interest rates. It was not intended to answer the question : Why is anyone willing to pay interest on a loan ? Keynes was taking it for granted that the dominant reason for borrowing is the expectation of profit on investment. Whatever the rate of interest charged for new borrowing may be, the opportunity cost of any one investment, from the point of view of the firm considering it, is the rate of profit obtainable on other investments. Thus, it is the rate of profit, not the rate of interest, that enters into the normal supply price of any particular commodity.

When normal prices obtain, each seller receives, over any

8

period, sums equal to the costs that he has incurred in production of the goods sold, including a notional charge for interest, at a rate equal to the ruling rate of profit, compounded over the interval from the moment when cost was incurred to the moment of receiving payment. Products enter into the production of each other and producers are selling to each other ; the number of stages into which the chain of operations is divided makes no difference to the result. When one producer buys from another, he pays a price which includes the notional interest-cost up to date, and notional interest is added to that cost in obtaining the final price. When the intermediate product is part of his own output, notional interest is compounded on the costs that he incurs to produce it, over the period that it is passing through his hands. Thus the final sum of interest-cost is the same in either case.

The total net value of the output of all firms taken together over any period is the sum of final sales (cancelling out transactions between firms) *plus* the value of stocks in existence at the end of the period (including the value of long-lived equipment appropriately depreciated), *minus* the value of stocks (including equipment) in existence at the beginning of the period. This net value is equal to the wages and net profits earned in the period. The whole of the wages are paid out in money over the period (assuming that the interval of wage payments is sufficiently short) but part of the net profit accrues in the form of the increased value of stocks and equipment. In an uncertain world, both the calculation of depreciation and the valuation of stocks are full of puzzles, but their evaluation at normal prices on the basis of a given rate of profit is merely a matter of arithmetic. By the same token, the value of the stock of capital has an unambiguous meaning when the rate of profit is given.

Non-produced means of production, such as the 'land' of traditional theory, are a link between this model and the first one, in which supply and demand govern relative prices.[1] For the moment we assume them away in order to consider this model in a pure form.

---

[1] This is true also of qualitative differences in the supply of workers. See above, p. 7, note 2.

Where all means of production are produced within the economy and there are no economies or diseconomies attaching to the scale of production of particular commodities,[1] the normal prices corresponding to any level of the money-wage rate and rate of profit are determined by the technical conditions of production ; they are independent of the composition of output or the tastes of consumers. Demand has no effect whatever on relative prices. In Marshall's language, there is 'constant supply price' for each product (or set of joint products) taken separately, so that their relative prices in terms of each other and the price of labour-time in terms of each, cannot vary with their rates of output. Where there are a variety of methods of production available for any one commodity, the rate of profit determines which will be chosen, the proportions in which means of production of various kinds are used being adjusted accordingly. This system of prices was set out in mathematical terms by von Neumann ;[2] its operation is clearly exposed in Sraffa's *Production of Commodities by Means of Commodities*.

The difference between this system of prices and the Walrasian system is that here the equilibrium stock of means of production is determined by the flow of output, given the technical conditions and the rate of profit, whereas in the Walrasian system there is an arbitrarily given stock of means of production and outputs are determined by the technical and psychological conditions which govern the pattern of supply and demand.

The Rate of Profit

Technical conditions and the rate of profit determine the pattern of normal prices, including the price of labour-time in terms of each commodity ; money-wage rates determine the

[1] Economies and diseconomies to firms are quite a different story. There must be an appreciable minimum efficient size for a plant in each line of production (otherwise workers could scrape up enough credit to become self-employed). There need be no maximum efficient size for a firm. But if there is, we must suppose that capital gets itself organised into optimum-sized firms. A shortage of managers, permitting diseconomies of scale to individual firms, is akin to scarcity of natural resources and belongs rather to the first type of model.

[2] 'A Model of General Economic Equilibrium', *Review of Economic Studies*, vol. xiii (1945–46).

corresponding money price level. But what determines the rate of profit ?

Marx closes his system sometimes (following Ricardo) by postulating a real-wage rate governed by the conventional standard of life (the value of labour-time), and sometimes by taking as given the share of net profit in the value of net output (the rate of exploitation). Marshall conceals the problem behind a smoke-screen of moral sentiments. The latter-day neoclassicals are for ever chasing definitions round a circular argument. Sraffa offers no observations on the subject. Von Neumann postulates a real-wage rate which is precisely specified in terms of particular quantities of particular commodities. This solves the problem, but leaves us helpless when that assumption is relaxed. The question of what determines the normal rate of profit, when the real-wage rate is not to be taken as given, is a huge blank in traditional economic teaching.

To introduce Keynesian conceptions into the argument carries us a long step forward. There is an equilibrium relationship between net saving and net income. When equilibrium prevails, the total size and the distribution of net income are such as to satisfy the condition that net saving per annum is equal to the value of net investment per annum. In the short period, to which the formal argument of the *General Theory* was confined, the equalisation of saving to investment comes about mainly through varying the level of utilisation of given capital equipment; that is, through varying the level of total income. In long-run competitive equilibrium the relation of total income to the stock of capital is determined within certain limits by technical conditions (it varies with the rate of investment, but not necessarily in such a way as to assist in bringing savings into line). The distribution of income, however, is strongly influenced by the rate of investment.

From any stream of net income, the volume of expenditure for consumption will be greater the greater the share going to wage earners ; the proportion of saving is greater in incomes derived from net profits than in incomes derived from wages. Whatever the ratio of net investment to the value of the stock capital may be, the level of prices must be such as to make the distribution of income such that net saving per unit of value of capital is equal to it. Thus, given the propensity to save from each type of income (the thriftiness conditions) the rate of profit is determined by the rate of accumulation of capital.[1]

The assumption that wage earners do not save is a great simplification, but the argument does not depend upon it. If wage earners save, there must be a class of families who derive income both from work and from property. There are then four classes whose propensity to save has to be considered. Wage earners without property, the intermediate mixed class, rentiers (including shareholders) who do no work, and firms who retain part of net profits. The ratio of saving to income is a function of its distribution between these classes and of the propensity to save of each, which may be influenced by the distribution of property between families within them and the size of firms. There may be some direct influence of the rate of return obtainable on rentier wealth upon the propensity to save of each class. And the pattern of prices of commodities may also affect it. But these influences are secondary, and they may go either way. The main weight of the equalisation of savings to investment (at normal prices) falls upon the distribution of income between classes. The level of normal prices has to be such that the rate of profit is such that the distribution of income is such that the ratio of saving to the stock of capital is equal to the rate of accumulation.

[1] If, for the sake of argument, we assume that the ratio of net saving to net income, s, is independent of the distribution of income between wages and net profits, then the rate of accumulation, g, is a function of v, the ratio of value of capital to net income, $g = s/v$. With given technical conditions, v varies with the rate of profit — a higher rate of profit means that less capital-using techniques are chosen, and this generally (though not necessarily) entails a lower capital/income ratio. The amount of play in this ratio is limited, unless technical conditions are very plastic. Thus when s is given, there is only a certain range of possible rates of growth which are compatible with equilibrium at normal prices. Harrod not only takes the share of saving in income as given but also postulates that the rate of profit is somehow settled in advance; with a given spectrum of possible techniques, the rate of profit determines the capital/income ratio. Thus, for Harrod, s/v is determined independently of g. There is then only one value of g (the 'warranted rate of growth') that is compatible with equilibrium. When the actual rate of growth is less than this 'warranted' rate, the realised rate of profit is below the postulated equilibrium level, which pushes the actual rate still lower. Vice versa when the actual rate is above the 'warranted' rate. This knife-edge is created by the postulate that the equilibrium rate of profit is determined independently of the rate of growth.

The question, then, is thrown forward from : What determines the rate of profit ? to : What determines the rate of accumulation of capital ?

The Rate of Growth

Here also there is a blank in traditional teaching. The point of view embodied in the acceleration principle suggests that investment keeps up with the expected rate of growth of sales. But the rate of accumulation is itself the main determinant of the rate of growth of income, and therefore of sales. Carrying itself by its own bootstraps is just what a capitalist economy *can* do.

The notion that a firm invests so as to maximise annual profit to the firm belongs to a kind of model that is a cross between the two that we are discussing. A firm, in this type of analysis,[1] is an entity representing some kind of unit of entrepreneurship attached to the production of a particular commodity, like the artisans of the first model ; but unlike them it can both borrow indefinitely and employ as much labour as it likes. It enjoys diminishing returns from the application of hired factors to itself and it wishes to grow up to the size at which the marginal return on further investment is no greater than the marginal cost of borrowing. This structure, which is shaky enough even on its own ground, depicts the size which firms wish to attain. It says nothing about the rate of growth of existing firms or of the conditions in which new firms come into existence. It cannot pretend to say anything about the general rate of accumulation in the economy as a whole.

The 'supply of investible resources' is no guide, for accumulation generates the savings it requires. The limit to this process is set by the level to which it is possible to force down real wages. In any given state of affairs an upper limit to the possible rate of accumulation is set by the 'inflation barrier' which comes into operation when a fall in real wages is being resisted by raising money wages. Short of this limit, the supply of investible resources is whatever is required by the rate of accumulation.

Nor does the 'supply of loanable funds' provide a clue, for here also the bootstraps operate. A firm which owns capital

---

[1] To which I must admit to having contributed in my time.

can pledge it to borrow more. A higher rate of accumulation means a greater flow of profits and so both a greater amount of self-finance and greater borrowing power. The rate of accumulation, below the level set by the tolerable minimum of real-wage rates, can be whatever it likes. (This does not, of course, mean that a *rise* in the rate of accumulation in an economy, above what it has been in the past, meets no obstacles. It only means that the supply of finance does not prescribe what the normal rate of accumulation must be.)

Does the rate of growth of the labour force provide an answer? In von Neumann's system the labour force and the stock of capital grow at the same rate. This is because he has postulated that the excess of net product over the necessary real-wage bill is always invested, and the supply of workers grows as required so long as the necessary wage is provided for them.

No doubt there is a connection between the rate of growth of population and the standard of life but it is unreliable and apt to go in the contrary direction. We must allow the growth of the labour force to follow its own path. Should we then postulate that the stock of capital tends to grow in step with it, in such a way that a constant ratio of employment to population is always preserved, with a constant ratio of capital to labour? That is easy enough to postulate, and if we do so, the model is neatly closed. The autonomous rate of growth of the labour force determines the rate of accumulation. Given thriftiness conditions, the rate of accumulation determines the rate of profit. The rate of profit, given the technical conditions, determines the normal prices of all commodities and the value and physical composition of the equilibrium stock of capital per man.

This is easily said, but where is the world that it is supposed to describe? When did the right stock of capital come into existence, and what mechanism, supposing that it did, keeps accumulation going at the right rate? The argument of the *General Theory*, which shows that there is no such mechanism in a private-enterprise economy, cannot be true at each moment of time and yet untrue 'in the long run'.

The argument is sometimes advanced that evidence shows that, in reasonably prosperous countries, the percentage of unemployment is never seen to vary very much, averaging good times with bad, over the long run. This would only show, if it were true, that harmony between the rate of growth of population and the rate of accumulation is possible. The countries in which the latter is lower than the former are not amongst those that are reasonably prosperous. But even for prosperous countries the evidence is largely an optical illusion. Capitalist industry does not employ the whole work force in any country. Domestic service, paid or unpaid, jobbing work and small-scale trade, and, in most countries, agriculture, hold a reservoir of labour which fills up when regular employment is not expanding as fast as the population. The question of whether people are happier in these occupations than they would be in regular employment is not to the purpose. The point at issue is that there is no justification for putting an assumption into the model to make the rate of growth of the labour force set a minimum to the rate of accumulation.

Nor should we assume that it sets a maximum. When the rate of accumulation is faster than the rate of growth of the labour force and the system has run up against a scarcity of labour, it is the assumption of constant technical conditions that must give way. The firms in this situation are eager to raise output per man, even if they have to increase capital per man to do so. In the process they make innovations, and they are just as likely to end up with a lower capital/output ratio as a higher one.[1]

The fact of the matter is that there is no way to close the model that is both neat and plausible. We must be content to leave it open. To account for accumulation, we have to fall back upon human nature and the structure of society. Firms

---

[1] The notion of 'deepening the capital structure' as a necessary result of accumulation at full employment seems to be connected with a misapplication of the idea of a production function. At any moment, with given technical knowledge and given prices, there may be a spectrum of possible techniques available to choose from. Firms undertaking new investment at that moment choose those that promise the best rate of profit. The spectrum can be presented in a simplified form as a schedule showing techniques requiring less labour per unit of investment as having lower net value of output per unit of investment. These techniques all coexist at a moment of time. As investment goes on through time, the eligible techniques change, and there is not the smallest reason to identify the succession of techniques chosen with points on the schedule existing at one particular date.

once established have an urge to grow, or, at least, an urge to resist the encroachments on their markets of others who are striving to grow, and in each generation new men who own wealth or command credit have an urge to try their fortune. Amongst them, the overall rate of accumulation somehow emerges. To see why it is greater in some nations or at some dates than at others, we must delve into questions that are below the level at which the model is built.

Unsteady Growth

The model need not be confined to the case of produced means of production. To introduce scarce factors into it is easy enough, in principle,[1] so long as we stick to a comparison of equilibrium positions. Further categories of incomes, receipts of rent, earnings of rare natural abilities, etc., enter into the thriftiness conditions. The supplies of the factors in physical terms enter into the technical conditions. As before, there is an equilibrium pattern of prices corresponding to a given rate of profit, and a rate of profit corresponding to a given rate of accumulation. On this basis we can compare equilibrium positions with greater or less scarcity of particular factors of production.

But then, as in the last model, the mere fact of accumulation going on is changing the equilibrium pattern of prices, for the stock of some kinds of means of production is accumulating and of others not. When population and equipment are increasing but 'land' is not, classical diminishing returns are in operation and rents rising as time goes by. Once more, the assumption of constant technical conditions becomes untenable. Investment in substitution for 'land', and in exploring for new supplies (as well as 'land'-saving improvements in methods of production), are stimulated by growing scarcity. There is no reason to expect a balance of supply and demand to be maintained. From time to time the growth in supply takes a long jump ahead of the growth in demand, so that relatively short periods of high normal prices for the commodities depending upon natural resources are followed by relatively long periods

---

[1] I have attempted a sketch, on very simple assumptions, in *Accumulation of Capital*, Book VI. Sraffa (*op. cit.* chap. xi) discusses it in terms of a constant composition of output at different rates of profit.

of low normal prices while demand is catching up. We must therefore carry over from the last model the conclusion that equilibrium prices are never likely to be ruling at any particular moment.[1]

On top of this there is another source of disturbance. Equilibrium today implies that there has been correct foresight in the past about what today would be like, so that the composition of the stock of capital today is appropriate to the rate of profit and the composition of output obtaining today. The absence of foresight makes it necessary to bring into the argument the whole Keynesian analysis of how an economy reacts to changes in the 'state of the news' in an uncertain world.

There are two more jokers in the pack — the price policy of firms (Kalecki's 'degree of monopoly'), which has an important influence upon the thriftiness conditions ; and money-wage rates, which can follow their own history more or less independently of what is happening to the equilibrium position in real terms, and which can react upon the real position by changing the distribution of real incomes, affecting expectations and influencing the supply of finance.

The analysis of the meaning of normal prices must certainly not be taken as a prediction that normality will be a usual state of affairs.

A MODEL FOR THE FUTURE

Technical progress is not only induced by scarcity of labour, it partly comes about through the mere accumulation of knowledge. Consider an economy in which a continuous autonomous rise in productivity is going on. For simplicity we will assume that technical progress is neutral in the sense that a constant labour force, divided in constant proportions between the tasks of producing commodities for sale to consumers and of maintaining a stock of ever-improving means of production (including equipment to produce equipment and teachers to train designers), produces an ever-increasing flow of output. For this system to keep running (from an initial position in which

[1] It is absurd, though unfortunately common, to talk as though 'in the long run' we shall reach a date at which the equilibrium corresponding to today's conditions will have been realised.

the stock of means of production is appropriately balanced) three things are necessary. The firms must have a sufficient appetite for increasing productive capacity to keep a constant labour force employed in producing means of production. The distribution of purchasing power to consumers (workers, including teachers, managers, etc., and rentiers, including shareholders) must be such as to permit consumption to grow at the same rate as capacity output. (This may come about with constant prices through money-wage rates and money dividends increasing at that rate, or through a fall in selling prices relatively to money incomes.) Finally, the consumers must actually spend on the products of industry at such a rate as to keep demand expanding in step with capacity output.

When the first condition is not fulfilled, employment offered by industry is declining. The unemployed scratch up a living as best they may. When the second condition but not the third is satisfied (industry distributes enough income but the income receivers do not want to spend it on the products of industry), the unemployed can make a living by selling their services to the beneficiaries of industry.

In our second model the whole emphasis was on organised employment, workers surplus to the requirements of industry were treated as living in unemployment, more or less disguised ; equipment was treated as an adjunct to labour ; and the money-price level was governed by the money-wage rate. Such a model is not appropriate to an economy in which the self-employed are an important and reasonably productive part of the total population.

Let us consider an economy in which employment of labour in organised industry has become vestigial. There, output is produced by robots and by experts who design robots to produce robots. The experts are produced by self-reproducing educational establishments maintained out of the profits of the firms which own and operate robots. The robot firms are legally owned by shareholders but in effect controlled by managers. The households of shareholders, managers, experts and teachers draw income from the robot firms. The rest of the population is self-employed, making a living by selling services to the other households and amongst themselves.

The Small Businesses

The self-employed are organised in small businesses. They buy consumer goods and equipment (hair-driers, washing machines, etc.) from the robot sector. (To get started, a young man must take service in a business already in being ; in a short time he sets up on his own ; thus the amount of employed labour remains small. To retain a hired worker it would be necessary to pay as much as he expects to earn on his own and since economies of large scale to the individual business are inappreciable, this would leave no margin of profit.)

The self-employed resemble the peasants and artisans of the first model in that, for them, the distinction between saving and consumption does not arise. They spend all they get, either in consumption or on equipment. (Loans that they obtain from the robot firms are short-term, and the instalments for repayment may be regarded as a form of spending.) In another respect they are more like the capitalist firms in the second model—there are no inherited skills or natural factors of production. Anyone, given time, can learn any trade, and in long-run equilibrium the returns to a 'representative firm' are the same in every line. This sector of the model provides the setting required for Marshall's analysis of industries composed of family firms ; the details can be filled in accordingly.

The Robots

The robot sector, at any moment, is producing a flow of goods for sale, which depends upon the stock of robots that has been built up, the skill with which they have been designed, and the proportion of the stock devoted to maintaining and enlarging the stock. The firms, as such, buy only from each other. Taken as a whole, their outpayments are salaries and the dividends which they pay to shareholders who financed them when the stock of robots was being built up;[1] their receipts are the value

[1] The level of salaries must be high enough to prevent experts and managers from joining the ranks of the self-employed and not so high as to cause shareholders to sell out and invest in having their sons trained as experts. Between these limits the level of salaries is a matter of convention, bargaining power and competition between firms. There is also an element of convention or historical accident in the money value of dividend payments.

of their sales. To avoid some complications, we will postulate that there are no savings, on balance, from the incomes paid out by the robot firms. Part of these incomes are spent on consumer goods produced by robots and part on the services of the self-employed. The latter spend all they get either on the products of robots or on each other. Their total income is thus related by a multiplier to the payments they receive from the robot sector, and the value of their purchases from it are equal to what they are paid by it. The receipts of the robot firms are thus equal to their payments. This settles the price level for a given volume of saleable output.

The normal relative prices of various commodities are determined, as in the last model, by the rule that there is an equal rate of expected profit on investment in each type of robot.[1] The flow of output of saleable products is increasing from year to year at a rate depending upon the skill of the experts in improving the design of robots and the rate at which the stock is increasing. (Both product and stock of robots must be valued on the basis of a chain-index to allow for the introduction of new types.) Prices remain constant when money payments by the robot firms are increasing at the same rate as the output of saleable goods. When money payments rise faster, there is a rise of prices which is diffused also through the self-employed sector. When money payments rise less fast, if the robot firms continue to sell their capacity output, prices fall and the self-employed enjoy an improvement in their terms of trade. If the robot firms maintain prices instead of permitting them to fall, capacity output cannot be sold; it ceases to be worth while to maintain the stock of robots and the system falls into stagnation.

---

[1] Since there are no wages, the rate of profit is identical with the ratio of net output to the stock of robots. There are some standard physical elements (say, nuts and bolts) that enter into the production both of robots and of saleable goods. This tethers the normal prices of robots to those of saleable goods, and makes it possible to value net product and the stock of robots at normal prices. (Cf. Sraffa, *op. cit.*) When technical progress is improving the design of robots, output per unit of input is rising as time goes by, and with it the rate of profit. Profits paid out as dividends are spent (directly or via the self-employed) on the products of robots. The rising rate of profit can then be said to be due to a constant rate of accumulation combined with a rising propensity to consume.

The last case (in which incomes fall but prices do not) shows how easy it is, in this model, for the economy to be let down by its bootstraps. It is interesting to observe that in this case a failure of effective demand does not cause unemployment. In the robot sector there are no workers employed (the experts, we may suppose, continue to draw salaries though no longer exerting themselves to the full) and the self-employed accept a fall in real income and continue to offer their services for what they will fetch.

The queer appearance of this model is due to the fact that it represents an economy in which conventions and rules are being observed after they have ceased to be appropriate to the technical situation. The shareholders are continuing to receive the 'reward of abstinence' although their only function in the economy is to spend money.

CONCLUSION

Analysis of current problems cannot wait until models (of which these three are only a sample) have been properly worked out, the appropriate mixture selected and the interaction between them properly diagnosed. More rough-and-ready methods have to be used. All the same, simplified models can perhaps help towards an understanding of the nature of real problems, provided that their own nature is properly understood. They can certainly hinder when it is not understood.

II

A MODEL OF ACCUMULATION

CLOSED AND OPEN MODELS

CONSIDER the most familiar piece of economic analysis : on the plane surface of the page of a text-book two curves are drawn, representing the flow of supply of a commodity per unit of time and the flow of demand for it, each as a function of price. They cut at the point E, where price is OP (on the y axis) and quantity traded OQ (on the x axis). We are accustomed to say that this represents a stable position of equilibrium if, at prices above CP, the supply curve lies to the right of the demand curve. What does this stability of equilibrium mean ? Clearly it means that E is a possible, and the only possible, position of equilibrium in the situation depicted by the curves. Does it mean any more than that ? It is often said that the picture shows that when price is above OP, it tends to fall towards E, and when it is below, to rise towards E. But this is by no means either clear or convincing.

First of all, falling and rising are movements in time, and there is no time on the plane surface of the diagram. Time may be conceived to lie at right-angles to the page but nothing in the picture tells us what happens when we move off the sheet.

Moreover, if price is anywhere but OP, it shows that expectations are not being fulfilled. Equilibrium means that the market price has settled at the supply price of the quantity being sold ; sellers are offering the quantity OQ in the expectation of selling at this price. If the price has recently risen above what was expected, it may very well have caused expectations to be revised in a way that will send it higher. Or if it has been falling, it may very well be going, not towards OP, but past it.

Now a pendulum is brought into the argument. The point E is said to be like the vertical position of a pendulum. The pendulum may be said to be *tending* towards the vertical even at those moments when it is moving away from it.

This metaphor can be applied to a market in which there is a clear concept in the minds of dealers as to what the equilibrium position is. In such a case it is true to say that price is always *tending* towards equilibrium even if it never settles there, and that, once settled, it will return to the equilibrium position after any chance displacement. For, in this case, dealers believe that profit is to be made by selling when price is above *OP* and buying when it is below.

How could they come by a belief that *OP* is the equilibrium price ? From experience. But the experience of each one is the result of how the others behave. The curves in the diagram are nothing but a statement of how buyers and sellers are assumed to behave.

What meaning can we attach to the conception of a position which is never reached at any particular moment of time but yet which exists only in virtue of the fact that the parties concerned believe, at each moment of time, that it will be reached in the future ?

The way out of this puzzle is to recognise that there are two kinds of economic argument, each of which is useful in analysis provided that it is not stultified by being confused with the other.

Logical and Historical Time

One kind of argument proceeds by specifying a sufficient number of equations to determine its unknowns, and so finding values for them that are compatible with each other (as above, the supply curve and the demand curve determine compatibility of price with quantity traded). The other type of argument specifies a particular set of values obtaining at a moment of time, which are not, in general, in equilibrium with each other, and shows how their interactions may be expected to play themselves out.

The first type of argument is not confined to stationary equilibrium relations. The equations may determine a path through time—say a continuous accumulation of capital, or a particular pattern of fluctuations. But the time through which such a model moves is, so to speak, logical time, not historical time.

To take a familiar example, in a model applicable to a pure competitive private-enterprise economy, the equations may show constant employment ; a relation between value of capital per man and value of output per man (values being reckoned in terms, say, of a basket of commodities—that is, goods sold to consumers[1]) that implies a rate of profit on capital falling as the total value of capital increases ; and a relation between savings and profits that implies a rate of accumulation falling as the total value of capital increases. This describes a process in which capital is continually increasing at a decelerating rate. The model is following a path in logical time approaching in one direction a 'future' state with some limiting value of the rate of profit and in the other a 'past' state of indefinitely rapid growth.[2]

Drawing the movement with 'time' from left to right across the page and the rate of output of commodities vertically, there is a ceiling showing the output compatible with zero accumulation (equilibrium in the stationary state corresponding to our equations) and a curve asymptotic to it representing the path that the model follows as the value in terms of commodities of the stock of capital goods grows.

We can if we like chop the curve into lengths and present a number of sections in the same 'period', each with a different value of capital. That with the smallest value of capital is accumulating fastest 'today', but by the time it reaches the value of capital which one above it enjoys 'today', it will have slowed down to the rate of accumulation that that economy is experiencing 'today'. Each is following the same path from an indefinitely remote past towards a future that it will never reach.

Now, it is a nonsense question to ask : Is such a path stable, so that if the economy were displaced by some chance event, it would return to the path again ? The reason why it is a nonsense question is as follows. Equilibrium implies that each

---

[1] Services sold to consumers are left out of the argument, for simplicity.
[2] Cf. my 'Accumulation and the Production Function', *Collected Economic Papers*, vol. ii, and *Economic Journal*, September 1959.

firm has arranged its affairs so as to maximise its own profits. This requires that firms carrying out accumulation should have sufficient foresight to pick in advance the forms in which investment will be embodied suitably to the market situations that will be met with in the relevant 'future'. (In general, more mechanised techniques and longer processes of production are chosen at a lower rate of profit.) If, at any moment, the actual position were appreciably off the prescribed path, they would not have made the right choices ; equality between the expected and the actual level of profits would not obtain. But if this has happened, we are in a world where it is liable to happen. A world in which expectations are liable to be falsified cannot be described by the simple equations of the equilibrium path. The out-of-equilibrium position is off the page, not in the same era of logical time as the movement along the path.

A large part of traditional economic argument is concerned with relations between prices, outputs, the rate of profit and so forth, in an economy existing in the conditions that prevail at the ceiling ; that is, in a stationary state. The argument consists of comparing the stationary states belonging to different sets of equations ; marginal productivity, comparative costs, profit-maximising monopoly price and many other familiar concepts, belong to this department of analysis.

There is much to be learned from *a priori* comparisons of equilibrium positions, but they must be kept in their logical place. They cannot be applied to actual situations ; it is a mortal certainty that any particular actual situation which we want to discuss is not in equilibrium. Observed history cannot be interpreted in terms of a movement along an equilibrium path nor adduced as evidence to support any proposition drawn from it.

A model applicable to actual history has to be capable of getting out of equilibrium ; indeed, it must normally not be in it. To construct such a model we specify the technical conditions obtaining in an economy and the behaviour reactions of its inhabitants, and then, so to say, dump it down in a particular situation at a particular date in historic time and work out what will happen next. The initial position contains, as well as physical data, the state of expectations of the characters concerned (whether based on past experience or on traditional beliefs). The system may be going to work itself out so as to fulfil them or so as to disappoint them.

In a model depicting equilibrium positions there is no causation. It consists of a closed circle of simultaneous equations. The value of each element is entailed by the values of the rest. At any moment in logical time, the past is determined just as much as the future. In an historical model, causal relations have to be specified. Today is a break in time between an unknown future and an irrevocable past. What happens next will result from the interactions of the behaviour of human beings within the economy. Movement can only be forward.

An initial position might happen to be in near-enough equilibrium (at least we can imagine it to be so for the sake of argument) in the sense that no one in the economy who has any power to change his behaviour (to alter prices, purchases, techniques of production or what not) desires to do so. Then it is not nonsense to ask whether the position is stable, in the sense that a chance departure from it would quickly be reversed. (In this sense the equilibrium position in the market for a commodity is stable when dealers have a clear view of what the equilibrium price for that commodity is.)

An economy may be in equilibrium from a short-period point of view and yet contain within itself incompatibilities that are soon going to knock it out of equilibrium. (For instance, an expectation that the prices ruling in a seller's market are going to last may be inducing investment in productive capacity that will bring the seller's market to an end.) Or it may be in equilibrium also from a long-period point of view so that the position will reproduce itself, or expand or contract in a smooth, regular manner over the future, provided that no external disturbance occurs. The path that the model then follows appears exactly like the equilibrium path, but it is still an historical, causal story that has to be told—the economy follows the path because the expectations and behaviour reactions of its inhabitants are causing it to do so.

When the initial conditions are not in equilibrium, the model depicts how their interactions will play themselves out over the next future. When a disturbance occurs on the equilibrium path, the model depicts how the economy responds to it. In reality, disturbing events occur on disequilibrium paths. The resulting turbulence is beyond the skill of model builders to analyse. Historical analysis can be made only in very general terms. When the analysis leads to results that are contradicted by experience the model must be re-examined to see whether there was some error in its construction or only some ill-considered application of it in the analysis.

The vice of the 'vulgar economics' that dominated academic teaching before Keynes (and still flourishes in some fields) was in drawing practical conclusions from equilibrium analysis.

When we compare equilibrium positions, that with a larger labour force has more employment—because full employment is specified as a characteristic of equilibrium; no causal mechanism is specified to show how an increase in the labour force raises the demand for labour in organised industry. When we compare points on an equilibrium path, that with the fastest rate of growth has the highest ratio of saving to consumption; this does not mean that thriftiness is propitious to accumulation. In equilibrium, the rate of interest cannot be greater than the rate of profit on investment, for if it were, decumulation would be going on. This does not mean that a fall in the rate of profit produces an equivalent fall in the rate of interest. When we compare short-period situations, in competitive conditions, with the same physical equipment, that with the lower level of employment has the higher level of real wages per man hour, for, if it were not, the competitive prices cannot be ruling. This does not mean that raising wages causes unemployment.

On all these points, when challenged by Keynes, orthodox economists started looking round for causal relations that would establish the theorems that had been illegitimately deduced from equilibrium analysis. A bastard generation of theorems emerged—such as that, with unemployment, money-wage rates fall so that, provided the quantity of money is not reduced, the rate of interest is lowered, and (an unstated proviso, which has only to be stated to appear ridiculous) if expectations of profit in money terms are unaffected by the fall in prices, investment will increase. In these theorems (which continue to proliferate)

Keynesian causal relations are fitted into an arbitrary set of assumptions fixed up so as to lead to the results once believed to be established by equilibrium analysis.

A curious feature often found in the exposition of these pseudo-causal models is that equilibrium lies in the future. It is admitted that the economy today is not in an equilibrium position, but it is tending towards equilibrium and will get there in due course. There was evidently some influence in the past that prevented equilibrium from being reached so far, but the future is going to be different.[1]

It is also characteristic of the pseudo-causal models to throw up puzzles about the correct method of measurement of the quantities that enter into them. In concrete reality (as opposed to imaginary equilibrium conditions) the entities described as the amount of employment, the available labour force, the level of prices, the quantity of money, and so forth, are not sharply demarcated at the edges and are immensely complex in their internal structure. They can be presented, as Keynes used to put it, in a who's who of detailed items ; to express them as a number of homogeneous units we have to adopt some kind of convention, and each convention gives a different number for the same concrete situation. In a causal model the entities are of this vague and complex nature ; when simple measures are used, their conventional basis is frankly exposed. There is room for discussions about which convention is more in accord with common sense, but there is no meaning in a discussion about which is the correct one.[2]

In concrete reality an overall rise or fall in prices, employment, interest rates, or what not, is accompanied by relative changes in particular markets and regions, so that the pattern alters with the level. In a causal model these complications have to be recognised. When we are concerned with such a strong overall movement that any reasonable index would show

---

[1] A striking example of this kind of theorem is in Hicks, 'A "Value and Capital" Growth Model', *Review of Economic Studies*, June 1959, where correct foresight about the future is enjoyed today, but has not been enjoyed about today in the past.

[2] This point is clearly brought out in the account of Index Numbers in Chapter 8 of Keynes' *Treatise on Money*. What is there said about price indices applies, *mutatis mutandis*, to problems of measurement of all economic entities.

pretty much the same change, the shifting pattern may be neglected, but when the relative changes are important they play a part in the causal story itself.

In a pseudo-causal model in which there is a mechanism relating the quantity of money and the level of wages in such a way as to make the system tend towards a state of full employment, the money-wage rate, the level of prices, the rate of interest, the quantity of money and the rate of profit, must have precise meanings, for those are the entities which constitute the mechanism. How to match up these simple postulated entities with complex reality is an insoluble problem. But this is only to be expected, for the entities were not derived in the first place from contemplating reality ; they were hastily summoned out of their setting in a closed model only to try to recapture for equilibrium theory the position that Keynes had demolished.

The Rate of Profit

In a closed model applicable to a competitive economy in stationary equilibrium the rate of profit on capital (which may be zero) is that which is compatible with zero accumulation. Competition implies that the rate of profit is uniform throughout the economy. With given technical conditions and given money-wage rates, this determines the price of every commodity and of each component of the stock of capital goods. It thus determines the real-wage rate in terms of any basket of commodities and the cost of labour to each employer in terms of his own product. The rate of profit obtainable on each round of reinvestment of gross profit on replacement of capital goods is identical with the rate obtained on past investments.

In reality the situation today is not necessarily that which was expected when the relevant decisions were made in the past. The current rate of profit—that is, the ratio of current gross profits, minus depreciation, to the value of the stock of capital at current replacement costs—is not identical with the rate of profit which is expected to be realised on investments currently being made.

Both the realised rate of profit and the expected rate are vague and complex entities. The realised rate of profit is vague because there are various conventions that can be used to assess it. The expected rate is vague because of uncertainty. Both are complex because each is an amalgam of the variegated experience of a large number of firms.

The view which the firms take of what is properly to be regarded as current profit has an influence upon the distribution which they make to rentiers, and so influences effective demand for commodities (that is, goods and services sold to the public). It also has an important influence upon expectations and so affects investment plans.

In constructing an historical model it is necessary to distinguish between the current and the expected rate of profit, and to specify what is assumed to be the connection between them. When an historical model is imagined to be following a smooth path on which the rate of profit expected on investment has been constant for some time, and has in fact been realised, we may suppose that its inhabitants hold very confident expectations that the rate of profit on investments now being made will be equal to that realised in the past. Such a path will be stable if small discrepancies between realised and expected profits do not change expectations. Investment decisions are then not affected by chance changes in current receipts (there is no 'accelerator') and accumulation continues smoothly on its path until some basic change in conditions or some major chance event upsets it.

Where experience has been very varied, confident expectations cannot be held. In such conditions there is a propensity for present experience to be overweighted in the formation of expectations ; a chance change in current receipts then has an effect on investment decisions. The model follows a different course according as investment is assumed to be governed by the expectation that the current situation, whatever it may be, will continue indefinitely, that change will continue in the same direction, or that a departure from the average of past experience will reverse itself, partially or wholly, after a time.

The Quantity of Capital

The problem of measurement of a stock of capital has given a great deal of trouble. This has arisen from the habits of thought inculcated by pseudo-causal models. From the proposition that, in equilibrium conditions with identical technical possibilities, a larger ratio of 'capital' to labour is associated with a lower rate of profit and higher real wages, the pseudo-causal theorem is deduced that accumulation of capital tends to lower the rate of profit. It therefore becomes a matter of the greatest importance to determine what is meant by 'capital' in the equilibrium proposition.

When we take the proposition in its own setting, in a closed model, the meaning of 'capital', though somewhat complicated, is quite unambiguous.

In any one stationary position the stock of capital goods is being reproduced continuously, item by item, so that the who's who of physical capital goods is unchanged in quantity, specification and age composition. A uniform rate of profit rules throughout the economy and there is a constant level of money-wage rates, so that all prices are determined; and the value of the stock of capital, whether in terms of money, commodities or labour time, is perfectly unambiguous.

A favourite exercise in stationary equilibrium analysis is to compare positions which have access to exactly the same technical knowledge but which exist in equilibrium with different rates of profit. (An economy which is in stationary equilibrium with a lower rate of profit has more thrifty capitalists.) Where the rate of profit is lower the real-wage rate is higher.

Generally speaking (apart from certain cranky cases[1]) in the economy with a lower rate of profit more mechanised techniques of production have been selected. There is a different who's who of capital goods in each economy. A given difference in the rate of profit is associated with a smaller difference in real wages, the more responsive is technique to differences in real wages (the easier in a technical sense is the 'substitution of capital for labour').

Comparing two stationary equilibrium positions with different rates of profit, the who's who of capital goods may have few or no items in common, and there is no presumption that the more mechanised technique requires machines that weigh more (though there is a presumption in favour of longer

---

[1] See my *Accumulation of Capital*, p. 109.

life). This has given rise to all the trouble. There is no physical measure that reflects the difference in the capital/labour ratio. Nor is there any direct measure in terms of value. With a different rate of profit the pattern of relative prices is different, and there is no common measure of the value in terms of money or of commodities to apply to the two stocks of capital goods. A measure in terms of labour-time makes more sense, for there is a general presumption that a more mechanised technique involves a greater quantity of labour-time embodied in the stock of equipment. But even this measure is not free from ambiguities, for the time pattern of production has to be taken into account ; in equilibrium the cost of production of capital goods includes interest at a rate equal to the ruling rate of profit on the capital goods required to produce them. Man-hours alone are not an adequate measure. Nevertheless, the stock of capital goods is whatever equilibrium requires it to be. The difficulty is only about how to describe it.

The simplest method is to assume a uniform money-wage rate in the economies to be compared, and to draw up a schedule showing what the cost of each stock of capital goods would be at a uniform rate of profit. On this basis we can draw a *productivity curve* showing the permanently maintainable flow of output per head of commodities and the money (that is, wage unit) value of capital per head at each rate of profit. On any one curve the various degrees of mechanisation are shown in ascending order, that with a higher output per head requiring a higher capital/labour ratio. For each economy we pick out the technique of production in use there from the productivity curve corresponding to the rate of profit ruling there. Technique and rate of profit determine output per man employed and profit per man employed. They therefore entail the real-wage rate. We can now see for each economy the value of capital in terms of labour-time and in terms of commodities.[1]

There is no difficulty about this analysis so long as no conclusions are drawn from it. Economies with different rates of profit must exist either at different dates or in different regions. Between two dates technical knowledge has altered. Between two regions there are differences in natural and human resources.

[1] *Op. cit.* pp. 411-16 for diagrams illustrating the above.

A Model of Accumulation

The comparison of different economies with the same technical possibilities and different rates of profit is an exercise in pure economic logic, without application to reality.

In an historical model, the stock of capital goods at some base date is taken to be simply whatever it happens to be. It can be valued at historic cost or at current reproduction cost, or in terms of its prospective earning power discounted at whatever is considered to be the appropriate rate of interest. Each measure (unless, by a strange fluke, perfect equilibrium obtains) is vague and complex, and each gives a different result. This is certainly a very tiresome state of affairs for both private and social accountants, but it cannot be amended by pretending that it is not so.

Aggregation

A model which took account of all the variegation of reality would be of no more use than a map at the scale of one to one.[1] In order to examine large, overall movements within an economy or to compare economies each considered as a whole, we have to divide into broad groups the inhabitants, the organisations, the incomes and the products — workers and capitalists, firms and households, wages and profits, consumption goods and means of production and so forth. For a first sketch we may simplify the model by assuming a group homogeneous within itself — all workers alike, all firms alike, a single consumption good and so forth. In doing so, we must be careful not to make a simplification in such a way that the model falls to pieces when it is removed. For instance, we can measure a flow of output of consumer goods in adjacent periods of time or adjacent countries, for there is a large element of physically identical items in each output, and the rest can be measured in terms of it, on the basis of ruling market prices. This procedure may conceal serious flaws in a measure to be used in discussions of welfare or the standard of life of the population concerned, but it will serve, in a rough and ready way, for discussions of productivity provided that the common element in production is a substantial proportion of the whole. (It would not serve to compare the physical productivity of labour amongst, say, the

[1] Cf. Lewis Carroll, *Sylvie and Bruno*, p. 169.

33

Eskimos and the Trobriand Islanders.) For the reasons mentioned above, a similar measure of physical stocks of capital goods is not available.

A highly aggregated model is useful only for a first sketch of the analysis of reality, but it is much easier to fill in the details in the outline drawn by a simple model than it is to build up an outline by amassing details. The essays in this volume are concerned only to contribute towards clearing up the outline, which has fallen into much confusion in modern times.

CHOOSING A MODEL

To build up a causal model, we must start not from equilibrium relations but from the rules and motives governing human behaviour. We therefore have to specify to what kind of economy the model applies, for various kinds of economies have different sets of rules. (The *General Theory* was rooted in the situation of Great Britain in the 1930's ; Keynes was rash in applying its conclusions equally to mediaeval England and ancient Egypt.) Our present purpose is to find the simplest kind of model that will reflect conditions in the modern capitalist world. Whether pure competitive *laisser-faire* capitalism ever existed is open to doubt ; it certainly does not today. But we cannot understand the objectives and effects of national policies until we understand the operation of the 'free' economy that they attempt to modify. Our model, therefore, depicts a system in which production is organised by individual firms and consumption by individual households, interacting with each other without any overriding control.

The independent elements in the model must correspond with the features of reality which are given independently of each other, either by the brute facts of nature or by the freedom of individuals within the economy to decide how they will behave. In an uncontrolled capitalist economy, firms are free, within wide limits, to decide upon the amount and form of the investment that they will carry out, on price policy and on the proportion of profits distributed to shareholders. Property-owning families (rentiers, for short) have a fairly wide freedom, and workers' families a limited freedom, to decide upon their rate of expenditure for consumption. Owners of property have freedom to decide the form in which their wealth shall be held. Trade unions influence the level of money wages. Banks influence the supply of money. Starting from any initial situation the interactions of the independent elements in behaviour with each other and with the physical, technical conditions in which they operate, determine the level and movement of employment, outputs, prices, interest dates, real incomes and so forth, as time goes by.

The determinants of equilibrium may thus be grouped under these headings :

    (1) Technical conditions
    (2) Investment policy
    (3) Thriftiness conditions
    (4) Competitive conditions
    (5) The wage bargain
    (6) Financial conditions.

These determinants govern the flow of output, cost and price of each kind of product, and so the rate of profit on capital and the real wages per unit of labour.

In a state of equilibrium, the stock of capital goods must already be that which is appropriate to the expected level of costs and prices, in the sense that no firm can see any advantage in changing the form in which its capital is embodied, or has any desire to alter the amount of employment it is planning to offer ; for equilibrium to persist it must turn out that expectations were correct. Equilibrium, in this sense, involves past history. For an historical model, we want to be able to start in any position, whether equilibrium or not, and discuss what will happen next. To the above list of determinants, therefore, we must add :

(7) The initial stock of capital goods and the state of expectations formed by past experience.

The Determinants
These seven elements are in the main independent of each other. Under any head a change may be made without, so to say, asking

permission from any of the others. In economic affairs, however, causation is always circular, and no element is completely independent of what is happening to the rest.

We now consider what are the characteristics of the determinants to be postulated for a model designed to discuss, in very general terms, the growth of a pure private-enterprise economy, and what are the cross-connections between them.

Technical conditions.—The numbers and quality of the labour force, with its propensity to grow through time; the state of the industrial arts, with their propensity to be improved; and the supplies of natural resources, are, obviously, the most important determinants of production, but for the kind of analysis with which we are now concerned, in the main they must be taken simply as given. There are, however, cross-connections which have a very great influence on growth, between the level of investment and technical conditions ; investment in education and training may have an influence upon the character of the labour force ; investment in research has an influence on the growth of technical knowledge. Moreover, the same motives which make firms eager to grow, are likely to make them eager to increase productivity, especially in conditions of scarcity of labour ; and the same motives which make them compete with each other, make them eager to find ways of reducing costs.

To rule out a group of complications which require separate treatment we postulate an economy in which there are no scarce natural resources.[1]

Investment policy.—In setting up a model it is convenient to draw sharply distinctions which in reality are blurred by many border-line cases. In discussing consumption and accumulation it is convenient to postulate an economy in which there are no border-line cases between firms and households (such as peasant families) and no border-line cases between saving and spending (such as buying a house). Investment in productive capital, then, is entirely governed by decisions of firms.

The question of what governs the rate of accumulation that firms undertake is one on which there is no agreed doctrine in orthodox economics.[2] The formal structure of the *General Theory* embodies the proposition that the rate of investment

---

[1] See below, p. 74.   [2] Cf. p. 13.

tends to be such as to equate the marginal efficiency of capital to the rate of interest ; this, it must be admitted, was in the nature of a fudge. For a scheme of investment to be undertaken, the profit expected from it must exceed its interest-cost by a considerable margin to cover the risk involved. The prospective rate of profit on the finance to be committed can be reduced to equality with the relevant rate of interest only by subtracting a risk premium equal to the difference between them. To say that the required risk premium is low or high is then no more than saying that the propensity to invest is high or low.

Keynes did not take his own formalism seriously : 'Most, probably, of our decisions to do something positive, the full consequences of which will be drawn out over many days to come, can only be taken as a result of animal spirits — of a spontaneous urge to action rather than inaction, and not as the outcome of a weighted average of quantitative benefits multiplied by quantitative probabilities. Enterprise only pretends to itself to be mainly actuated by the statements in its own prospectus, however candid and sincere. Only a little more than an expedition to the South Pole, is it based on an exact calculation of benefits to come. Thus if the animal spirits are dimmed and the spontaneous optimism falters, leaving us to depend on nothing but a mathematical expectation, enterprise will fade and die.'[1]

It is not only a matter of the innate characteristics of human nature but also of the kind of behaviour that is approved by society. Capitalism develops the spirit of emulation ; without a competitive urge to grow, modern managerial capitalism could not flourish. At the same time there are costs and risks attached to growth that keep it within certain bounds. To attempt to account for what makes the propensity to accumulate high or low we must look into historical, political and psychological characteristics of an economy ; with that sort of inquiry a model of this kind cannot help us. It seems reasonably plausible, however, to say that, given the general characteristics of an economy, to sustain a higher rate of accumulation requires a higher level of profits, both because it offers more favourable odds in the gamble and because it makes finance more readily

---

[1] *General Theory*, pp. 161-2.

available. For purposes of our model, therefore, the 'animal spirits' of the firms can be expressed in terms of a function relating the desired rate of growth of the stock of productive capital to the expected level of profits.

Thriftiness conditions.—The simplest assumption to make about the relations between income and saving is that used by von Neumann ; there are two classes of income, profits and wages ; all wages are spent and all profits saved. At the other extreme, the distinction between classes of income is completely ignored and saving is taken to be whatever proportion of total net income individuals, taken one with another, desire to make it. The first approach makes saving depend entirely upon the type of income concerned. The second makes it depend entirely on individual preferences. The first appears more cogent. Our model leans towards it, but admits some element of the second.

The most important distinction between types of income is that between firms and households. Decisions concerning saving are made by both. The firms normally retain from gross profits something more than what they regard as the proper depreciation allowances required to keep their pre-existing capital intact. Since our model reflects the view that the central mechanism of accumulation is the urge of firms to survive and to grow, we may suppose that this policy in respect to distribution of dividends is framed in the interest of the firm as such rather than of the shareholders.[1] The firm has to balance the consideration that retained profits provide finance without any obligations attached to it, against the consideration that the market for its shares on the stock exchange depends very much upon the amount of dividends that it is expected to pay. In this respect each one is subject to some extent to the behaviour of the others, for if a convention is established that it is the safe

---

[1] The code of proper behaviour recommended by the Institute of Directors is as follows :

Boards who settle their dividend policy by asking the question 'How little can we pay in order to keep the shareholders quiet ?' fail to understand what their responsibilities are. The question *should* be 'What is the proper amount we need retain in the long-term interests of the company ?'

Standard Board Room Practice. Prepared by a Special Committee. Published by the Institute of Directors.

and reputable thing to distribute no more than a particular proportion of profits, the market cannot penalise any one for adhering to the convention.

The amount of interest that firms are paying at any moment is the result of the terms on which finance was raised in the past.

The ratio of net saving by firms to their profits, then, depends on three sets of factors—the procedures that they use in calculating depreciation ; the structure of their indebtedness, with the interest obligations attached to it ; and their policy in respect to dividends.

Households may be divided into those of pure rentiers, using that term in a wide sense to include shareholders (since there are no scarce natural resources in the model, and no government, the only form of income-yielding property is the obligations of the firms) ; those whose income is entirely derived from earnings ; and those whose income is partly earned and partly derived from property.

The latter class will be gradually growing if wage earners are saving enough to leave some property to their heirs. For many of the problems with which we shall be concerned it lightens the argument very much, without making any essential difference to it, if we assume that there is no net saving, on balance, from earned income. We also rule out social security payments and unemployment allowances. Workers as a whole live from the earnings of those who are employed.

Rentiers' families must have saved in the past, otherwise they would not be rentiers. Along with their wealth, they inherit the desire to preserve and augment it. Their propensity to save may be influenced by the distribution of wealth amongst them, by the age composition of families, by the return to be expected on placements, by prospects of changing prices, by the selections of commodities offered to them, the skill of salesmen in luring expenditure from them, and so forth, but for our purpose here it is sufficient to express it simply as the proportion of receipts that they regard it as normal and proper to save.

The normal proportion of total profits saved, then, depends upon two factors — the proportion of profits distributed by the firms and the proportion of their receipts that rentiers save. The proportion of profits saved being given, the ratio of saving to total net income depends upon the ratio of total profits to total income.

Savings equal to investment.—In Marshall's scheme of thought the rate of accumulation of capital in an economy was governed by the propensity to save of the households composing it. In the *General Theory* the rate of accumulation depends upon the decisions of firms concerning investment. This change of view on the mechanism of a capitalist economy gave rise to a confused controversy over the meaning of the proposition that saving is equal to investment.

This proposition can be interpreted as an accounting identity. When Y is the net income of a year, C value of consumption, I value of net investment and S of net saving, then to say

$$Y = I + C$$
$$Y = S + C$$
$$\therefore \ S = I,$$

is merely to lay out the headings for a set of columns of statistics. Net income and net investment must be defined in such a way as to be consistent with each other. Net saving is the excess of net income, so defined, over consumption, and this is identical with net investment. Any excess of value of net investment over saving by households is not only equal to the amount of undistributed profit but is actually identical with it, for what is counted as net undistributed profit is that part of net investment which is not covered by borrowing.

When the proposition is treated as a statement of equilibrium conditions, it means that whatever the rate of investment may be, the level and the distribution of income must be such as to induce the firms and households, between them, to wish to carry out saving at an equal rate. Whatever the capital/income ratio may be, the level of prices relatively to money wages is such, in equilibrium conditions, as to provide sufficient profits to call forth a rate of saving equal to the rate of net investment. That is to say that the rate of profit on capital is such as to make saving per unit of capital equal to the rate of accumulation.[1]

[1] This is true even when we do not make the convenient assumption of no net saving from earned incomes ; even if all households saved the same proportion of their receipts, there would still be additional saving represented by the retained profits of firms. Thus the ratio of saving to capital would still be an increasing function of the rate of profit.

A Model of Accumulation

A third way of taking the proposition about saving and investment is to follow the consequences of a change in the level of investment. When there is a higher level of outlay (money wages being constant) on gross investment, in one year than the last, there will follow an increase in the level of activity and the level of prices (relatively to money wage rates) which is at first less than is appropriate to the increase in gross investment; for the rise of profits takes some time to be reflected in greater dividends, and expenditure takes some time to be readjusted to changes in income. At any point in the process, saving and investment must be equal in the truistic sense, and at no point need they be equal in the equilibrium sense.

There may be a cross-connection between the thriftiness conditions and the rate of accumulation in so far as distribution policy of firms may be influenced by their investment plans. In so far as a higher rate of accumulation is associated with reduced distribution, it has a weaker effect in raising the rate of profit.

Competitive conditions.—The contrast between monopolistic and competitive prices is usually conducted in terms of static equilibrium analysis (or in that strange kind of analysis in which equilibrium will be attained in the future). It is not to our purpose to attempt a dynamic theory of monopoly, but it is important to observe that there is no necessary connection between monopoly in the market sense and the rate of growth. Some firms with a strong hold over particular markets may be full of 'animal spirits' and grow by continually opening up new lines. Some near-enough competitive industries may have sunk into a lethargic state of live-and-let-live, and have little urge to expand. Comparing one economy with another, that in which there is a large number of monopolistic firms, or in which prices are regulated by agreements between groups of firms, is not necessarily less dynamic or growing more sluggishly. On the other hand, monopolies, especially in lines of production which require a heavy minimum investment in long-lived plant, cannot but be anxious to avoid excess capacity. A cautious investment policy, from the point of view of the economy as a whole, is equivalent to a low state of 'animal spirits'.

However that may be, there is another aspect to monopolistic behaviour. A single firm or a price-fixing group which has a strong hold over the supply of a particular commodity which has no close substitutes finds demand inelastic to price. It is likely, then, to find it advantageous to keep profit margins high. Given the total flow of demand in money terms, this means that there is so much the less demand in other markets and more competitive firms have to be content with lower profit margins. The total of profits cannot be increased by raising prices, unless at the same time effective demand is increased.

An all-round rise of profit margins would not increase total profits unless it was preceded by a corresponding increase in gross investment or in distribution to rentiers (and if it were, the same increase in profit margins would have come about automatically in competitive market conditions). Its effect is to reduce sales ; more or less the same gross profit is earned in a smaller volume of output, with lower real wages, less employment and under-utilisation of plant. Conversely, a cut in margins increases the real-wage rate without reducing profits.

Market behaviour is also important in connection with the reaction of prices to different kinds of unforeseen change. In particular, a fall in effective demand produces a greater fall in prices and a smaller fall in output the more closely does price policy correspond (with given technical conditions) to the ideal of perfect competition.

The wage bargain.—For a large part of the argument it will be convenient to assume money-wage rates constant. There are two kinds of situations, however, in which money-wage rates must be free to rise. The first is when there is an excess demand for labour, in the sense that plant is available to carry out the investment decisions of firms and to meet the demand for commodities that investment is generating, but there are not enough hands to man it. The second is when (given technical conditions) the rate of investment, together with the consumption of rentiers that it generates, is at such a level as to depress the real wage below what workers are willing to accept (or below the level at which they can work efficiently), so that an irresistible demand for higher money wages makes itself felt.[1]

Finance.—There are two aspects of finance which we must take into account. The first is the structural pattern of the

[1] Cf. p. 13 above.

relation between the distribution of the urge to accumulate of firms and the distribution of borrowing power. This largely depends upon legal conditions (it was revolutionised by the institution of limited liability), the organisation of financial institutions, the attitude of rentiers towards risk and so forth. For purposes of our model it is best treated, along with the 'animal spirits' of the firms, as an element in the propensity to accumulate of the economy.

The second aspect of finance is the general level of interest rates, which, with any one structure of financial institutions and pattern of distribution of borrowing power, may be higher or lower according to the relation between the supply and demand for placements of various kinds, including the supply of money.

Our model is intended to represent pure private enterprise, but it is impossible to imagine a capitalist economy without an organised monetary system. But monetary systems are national and monetary policy is bound up with the problems of the balance of payments and exchange rates. A model of a closed system in which monetary policy, via the interest rate, controls the level of investment, is a kind of day-dream that economists delight in, but our model is not designed to pander to this indulgence.[1] We therefore chose assumptions which give monetary policy a very minor role.

Replacements are normally financed entirely, and net investment to a considerable extent, from gross retained profits. Firms are able to raise additional finance by selling bonds and equities to rentiers, and by borrowing from banks at the ruling rate of interest.

Rentiers hold their wealth in the form of obligations of the firms or in bank deposits.

The banks allow their total lending (and therefore the supply of money) to increase gradually, at a constant rate of interest, as total wealth increases ; but when there is a sharp rise in the

---

[1] In some passages in the *General Theory* Keynes indulged in this day-dream, but his main concern was, on the theoretical plane, to demonstrate that in a closed system the rate of interest could be controlled (a demonstration that was necessary because of the confusion between the rate of interest and the rate of profit that was then prevalent) and, on the practical plane, to protest against the policy of sacrificing home employment to the balance of payments. It was for these reasons that interest rates play such a prominent part in his argument.

demand for money such as occurs in inflationary conditions, they raise the rate of interest to a level which checks investment.[1]

These assumptions are intended to reduce the importance of monetary policy in the operation of the model to a minimum, except as a stopper to inflation.

Equilibrium Relations

When the composition of the stock of capital in existence is in harmony with the rate of growth that firms are prepared to carry out, so that an overall rate of gross investment per annum, rising from year to year at a steady rate, would bring about the same overall rate of growth of the stock of capital (maintaining the appropriate proportion between equipment for producing equipment and equipment for producing consumer goods) ; and when the expectations of firms about the future are in line with current experience, the expected rate of profit (the marginal efficiency of investment) being the same in all lines ; then our model is in a state of internal equilibrium for the time being. (This does not guarantee that the current growth rate can continue to be realised : situations where it can and cannot continue will be discussed below.)

The whole position, in real terms, is then determined by the rate of accumulation which is being carried out.

In such an equilibrium position there is a normal price for each kind of output, which is governed by its cost of production and marketing, including in cost notional interest at a rate equal to the rate of profit on investment. The price policy of firms is such as to establish the normal capacity operation of plant. There is then an interlocking system of prices in terms of wage units, each output paying for the labour that it requires, the intermediate products which enter into it (including amortisation of plant) and interest on the capital employed in

[1] Interest and dividends paid to rentiers constitute net income for the recipients ; interest paid to banks represents their gross receipts. In general, different amounts will return to the firms as demand for consumption goods from rentiers' outlay and from the outlays of banks via the expenditure of their employees. This sets up some complications which it is not worth while to explore. We rule them out by assuming that the saving out of interest is the same for the banking sector as for rentiers when the rate of interest is at its normal level, while, when the rate has been raised to check inflation, the whole of the additional interest receipts of the banks are saved.

producing and selling it. When the stock of capital is valued at normal prices, the rate of profit on capital is then equal to the rate of profit on investment.

The distribution of profits by firms and the expenditure of rentiers are in their normal relation to current profits. Profit per annum is equal to the value of net investment plus the value of rentier consumption. The rate of profit on capital is determined by the ratio of net investment to the stock of capital (the rate of accumulation) and the proportion of profits saved. The level of wages in terms of commodities is determined by the technical conditions and the rate of profit.

The level of prices in terms of money is determined by the level of money-wage rates, which is arbitrarily given. The rate of interest is arbitrarily determined by the banking system, and the stock of money is adjusted to the level of money wages and prices in such a way as to establish it.

When the expectations entertained in the relevant past about what the current situation would be are turning out to have been correct, the forms in which investment has been embodied are appropriate to the current position. At the moment when investment decisions are made, firms are often presented with a choice of alternative methods of production. In our model, profits are desired for the sake of growth rather than growth for the sake of profits, but firms are still conceived to be attempting to 'maximise profits' in the sense that, in respect to particular choices, they prefer a more profitable to a less profitable alternative. Thus, if there are a variety of techniques, already known, for carrying out a particular line of production, investment plans are assumed to be designed to embody the technique which promises the highest rate of profit on the finance committed (which may consist of new investment or a reincarnation of the capital recovered, through amortisation, from an earlier investment). Thus a condition for the internal equilibrium of the system to be realised is that no firm is making use of one technique where another would be yielding a higher rate of profit.[1]

---

[1] This condition can be stated in terms of traditional marginal productivity concepts—equilibrium entails that the marginal net product of labour to an employer is not less than the wage in terms of product, and the marginal

Short-period Equilibrium

The above position depends upon the assumption that the initial conditions are in harmony with the determinants of the system. When initial conditions are not in harmony we cannot make use of the notion of a rate of profit which is uniform throughout the system and we cannot value output and the stock of capital at normal prices. We have to fall back upon the who's who of physical products.

We measure the flow of output of commodities in 'baskets' of representative composition, and we divide the stock of capital equipment into two sectors—plant designed for the production of commodities to be sold to consumers and basic plant which can be used either for producing itself or for producing plant for the commodity sector.

Now consider the situation with given stocks of plant of each kind, with a rate of gross investment going on, decreed by decisions of the firms that have already been taken, and with a flow of receipts of rentiers determined by the profits of the recent past.

Employment in gross investment is then given. Employment in the production of commodities is determined by the flow of sales (and the flow of sales expected over the near future, which governs the flow of reproduction of work in progress); the flow of sales is governed by the flow of demand in money terms coming from households and the price policy of firms.

If the short-period situation that we are examining is one in which there has been a fall of effective demand in the recent past, firms may be working plant below designed capacity and still charging the 'full cost' prices at which they were earlier able to sell their normal capacity output. But let us suppose that competition (in the short-period sense) is sufficiently keen to keep prices at the level at which normal capacity output can be sold. If the situation is one in which demand is higher than was expected, a seller's market prevails

---

productivity of investment to a firm is not less than the rate of profit, but it is to be observed that the marginal products are evaluated at a given set of prices. This line of argument does not apply to the comparison between techniques chosen at different rates of profit. Cf. above, p. 32.

and capacity is being strained, but there is not very much play in it. Thus we may say that employment in the production of commodities is more or less closely determined by the available plant.

The flow of expenditure on the purchase of commodities is equal to the flow of outlay on wages *plus* a certain part (determined by distribution policy and the thriftiness of rentiers) of the net profits enjoyed by the firms in the recent past.

The price level of commodities per 'basket' is this total flow of expenditure divided by the rate of output of baskets in physical units.

This price, with the ruling money-wage rate, determines the real wage in terms of the consumption good and the total amount of gross profit from sales.

We have to consider how the situation in which the firms find themselves influences their plans for the future. This involves the whole question of the mechanism of fluctuations in a private-enterprise economy. At this stage in the argument we assume that expectations are based upon a simple projection of the current situation. On the basis of prices and wages ruling today, firms calculate the rate of profit to be expected on investment.

The central mechanism of our model is the desire of firms to accumulate, and we have assumed that it is influenced by the expected rate of profit. The rate of investment that they are planning for the future is, therefore, higher the greater the rate of profit on investment (estimated on the basis of current prices). Valuing the existing stock of capital on the basis of the same rate of profit, we can then express their plans in terms of a rate of accumulation.

The double-sided relationship between the rate of profit and the rate of accumulation now appears. The accumulation going on in a particular situation determines the level of profits obtainable in it, and thus (on the basis of the type of expectations which we have postulated) determines the rate of profit expected on investment. The rate of profit in turn influences the rate of accumulation. The rate of profit generated by a particular situation may be such as to induce a rate of accumulation greater or less than that which is actually taking place.

The Desired Rate of Accumulation

The first question to be discussed is the relation between the rate of profit *caused* by the rate of accumulation and the rate of accumulation which that rate of profit will *induce*, which may be found in the short-period situations which the chances and changes of history throw up. The various possible relations can be mapped out in a diagram.

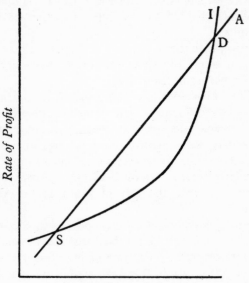

Rate of Accumulation

The *A* curve represents the expected rate of profit on investment as a function of the rate of accumulation that generates it. The *I* curve represents the rate of accumulation as a function of the rate of profit that induces it.

When the firms find themselves in a situation (to the right of *D* in the diagram) such that the rate of accumulation going on is higher than that which would be justified by the rate of profit that it generates, the investment plans being drawn up will bring a lower rate of accumulation into operation in the immediate future. The ratio of basic to commodity-sector plant is unduly high and further investment in it does not appear profitable ; the plans which the firms are now making will cause the ratio to fall.

When the current rate of accumulation is less than would be justified by the rate of profit that it is generating (the position lying between *S* and *D* in the diagram) the firms are planning to increase the rate of accumulation (unless there is some impediment to prevent them). The ratio of basic to commodity-sector plant is too low and (allowing for the replacements falling due) there is a higher ratio of basic plant in current investment than in the existing stock.

When the current rate of accumulation is at a level too low to generate profits sufficient to maintain even such a low rate, and any further fall would further increase the deficiency (the situation depicted by points below *S* in the diagram), the economy has fallen below its stalling speed and is heading towards even greater ruin and decay than it now suffers.

The point *D* represents a rate of accumulation which is generating just the expectation of profit that is required to cause it to be maintained.[1] This may be conveniently described as the *desired* rate of accumulation, in the sense that it is the rate which makes the firms satisfied with the situation in which they find themselves.[2]

The fact that the desired and the actual rate of accumulation coincide in a particular short-period situation does not by itself guarantee that they will continue to do so. There may be

[1] There is no logical necessity for the basic determinants to be such as to make all three types of situation possible. (1) The *A* curve may lie above the *I* curve all the way. There is then no limit to the desired rate of growth ; some physical obstacle has to be brought into the story to prevent the economy from exploding. (2) The *A* curve may lie above the *I* curve all the way below *D*. There is no intersection at *S* and no level of investment below which recovery towards *D* is impossible. (3) There may be an intersection at *S* but not at *D*. Then all possible rates of accumulation are divided between those below the stalling speed, which lead to ruin, and those above, which lead to explosive acceleration. (A case in which the *A* curve does not lie above the *I* curve anywhere in the positive quadrant of the diagram is impossible, for such an economy is not viable.)

[2] This concept is very similar to Harrod's *warranted rate of growth* and has a similar role in the analysis. Harrod, however, has never removed the ambiguity as to whether the firms are supposed to be content with the stocks of productive capital that they are operating or with the rate at which it is growing. To avoid confusion, it seems better to use a different term from his. Cf. below, pp. 33-5.

influences within the existing situation which will cause changes in the immediate future.

First, there is a lag between the receipt of profits and the rentiers' expenditure to which they give rise, so that a part of the current purchases of consumption goods are being made out of incomes derived from the distribution of profits of an earlier period. When the level of profits has not been growing smoothly, this is liable to cause wobbles in the relation between the current rate of accumulation and the current proceeds from the sale of consumption goods.

Second, past rates of accumulation leave fossils in the present structure of the stock of plant. When accumulation has been erratic in the past, the age composition of the stocks of the two kinds of plant will not be in a state of balance appropriate to the rate of accumulation that is now going on. From one short period to the next, the relation between current gross investment and net accumulation is then liable to be upset by a larger or smaller quantity of renewals falling due. Thus, having attained the desired rate of accumulation at one moment, the firms may be tipped off it at the next.

Before discussing such disturbances we will consider the development of the economy as it can be imagined to take place in tranquil conditions.

In a long run of time without disturbing events, the desired rate of accumulation (under the assumption about expectations that we are now making) will become established, if technical conditions permit. When accumulation has been going on for a sufficient time at the desired rate, the structure of the stock of productive capital has become more or less completely adjusted to requirements. Plants are divided between the sectors in near enough the proportions appropriate to the rate of accumulation which is taking place and the accompanying rate of consumption. The age-composition of the stock of plant, also, is a close approximation to that appropriate to the rate of growth ; each generation is larger than the last in more or less exact proportion to the growth rate of the economy. A rate of gross investment growing from year to year at the growth rate then generates net investment growing at very nearly the same rate, and so an almost perfectly steady proportionate growth in the physical stock of each kind of plant and working capital. Profit expectations are realised and so confirmed. The system is in a close approximation to the state of internal equilibrium described above, and remains in it while tranquillity continues to prevail.

DESIRED AND POSSIBLE GROWTH

We have been discussing the desired rate of accumulation for the firms as a whole which arises from the interaction of their individual plans under the proviso that there is no impediment to prevent them from growing as fast as they wish. We have said nothing about the availability of labour.

There are many interesting questions to discuss in relation to the influence upon the labour force of the age-composition of the population, the level of education and so forth, but we shall not enter into them here. We simply postulate a certain rate of growth of population, which may be zero, and assume that the available supply of labour grows with it, without any change in personal efficiency. The actual efficiency of labour, however, depends upon the state of technical knowledge. The formal analysis of technical progress is discussed below.[1] Here we shall merely assume that innovations are occurring throughout the economy in such a way as to be near-enough neutral on balance—that is, in such a way that the value of capital in terms of wage units per man employed does not alter appreciably when accumulation is going on at such a pace as to keep the rate of profit constant.

The rate of technical progress (the all-round rise in output per head that it produces) depends very much upon demand and supply of labour. When firms can see profitable markets expanding around them but cannot get hands, they set about trying to find labour-saving devices. (Since this occurs just as much in the production of equipment and intermediate products as in the final processes of production of commodities there is no reason why it should not be neutral on balance.) Without this stimulus innovations are more sluggish, and when there is a

[1] See p. 88 *et seq.*

surplus of labour, workers (with much support from public opinion) put up a resistance against the 'machines that take the bread out of their mouths'.

On the other hand, technical progress does go on even when there is massive unemployment. In practice it is not possible to distinguish sharply between 'autonomous' innovations due to the growth of knowledge, 'competitive' innovations due to the struggle between firms and 'induced' innovations due to the scarcity of labour, though in a rough-and-ready way the kind of situations that produce them can be observed.

For our present purposes it is sufficient to say that the desired rate of growth may fall short of the rate compounded of the growth of the labour force and the growth of output per head due to autonomous and competitive innovations ; a desired rate that is high relatively to the growth of the labour force may call forth the innovations that it needs ; or it may be so high that it cannot be satisfied and has to be restrained.

We now proceed to confront the desired rate of growth (resulting from the 'animal spirits' of the firms) with the rate of growth made possible by physical conditions (resulting from the growth of population and technical knowledge).[1]

I used the phrase 'a golden age' to describe smooth, steady growth with full employment (intending thereby to indicate its mythical nature). Corresponding nicknames may be given to other possible phases of growth.

A Golden Age

With a desired rate of accumulation equal to the possible rate, compounded of the rate of growth of population and of output per head, starting with near full employment and a composition of the stock of plant appropriate to the desired rate of accumulation, near full employment is maintained. This is a golden age.

The firms in our model are assumed (at this stage in the argument) to judge the future profitability of investment by current receipts, which implies that passing events, temporarily

---

[1] The following argument owes much to Harrod's distinction between the *warranted* and the *natural* rates of growth, but there are some important differences between his model and ours.

raising or lowering current receipts, produce the effect of an 'accelerator', one way and the other, on their investment plans; for the moment, however, we assume that conditions are sufficiently tranquil (and have been tranquil for a long enough past) to make such disturbances negligible; a steady rate of accumulation then rolls smoothly on its way. In so far as technical progress is raising output per head, the real-wage rate is rising equally. The rate of profit on capital remains constant. Techniques of production are chosen, at each round of gross investment, of the degree of mechanisation appropriate to the rate of profit, and gross profit margins are compatible with normal utilisation of plant.

From the point of view of the firms, *equilibrium* may be said to prevail, since the desired rate of accumulation is being realised. From the point of view of the overall demand and supply of labour *harmony* may be said to prevail. On the other hand, the position cannot be called an *optimum*; for the level of real wages depends partly upon the thriftiness conditions, so that there is an element in the situation of a conflict of interests between workers and rentiers. (A golden age in which there was no consumption out of profits would be an optimum, within the technical possibilities, from the point of view of the workers; the real-wage rate would be as high as was compatible with continuous full employment and the surplus accruing to capitalists would be no more than the necessary cost of maintaining it.[1])

A Limping Golden Age

A steady rate of accumulation of capital may take place below full employment. The stock of plant has the composition appropriate to the desired rate of accumulation, but there is not enough of it to employ the whole labour force.

The limp may be of various degrees of severity. When output is growing less fast than output per head, the level of employment in organised industry is falling as time goes by.

When output is rising faster than output per head, employment is increasing. It may be increasing faster than the labour force is growing (so that the system is heading towards full

[1] See below, p. 120 *et seq.*

53

employment) or more slowly so that the ratio of non-employed to employed workers is growing.

A Leaden Age

A growing ratio of non-employment means a falling standard of life for the workers all round, unless real wages for those employed are rising sufficiently rapidly to compensate for the rising ratio of mouths to employed hands (a somewhat implausible situation) or the opportunities for self-employment are sufficiently favourable.[1] When Malthusian misery checks the rate of growth of population, then, in the absence of technical progress, a situation might be reached in which the rate of accumulation and the rate of growth of the labour force were equal, the ratio of non-employment being great enough to keep the latter down to equality with the former.[2]

A Restrained Golden Age

We now turn to the more cheerful scene where, even with induced technical progress, it is impossible to maintain as high a rate of growth as firms are willing and anxious to carry out.

With a stock of plant appropriate to the desired rate of accumulation (which exceeds the rate of growth of population) and full employment already attained, the desired rate of accumulation cannot be realised, because the rate of growth of output per head (even with the stimulus of scarcity of labour) is not sufficient to make it possible.

There are two different ways in which it may be held in check.

When the firms desire to employ more labour than there is, a scramble for hands may lead to rising money-wage rates and consequently rising prices and a rising demand for credit to finance production. According to our assumptions, the rate of interest would then be pushed up to the point at which investment is checked. The demand for labour is thus prevented from exceeding the available supply.

[1] Cf. p. 19.
[2] This situation is different from that depicted by the 'iron law of wages'. In that case the growth of numbers is limited by a low level of real wages for those employed. Here it is limited as a result of the low rate of accumulation.

A Model of Accumulation

If the composition of the stock of plant had become adjusted to the physically possible rate of accumulation, leaving a sufficient margin of unemployment to prevent wages from rising, a sufficiently exact control of credit may be imagined to keep accumulation down to that level. (This is an aspect of the day-dream referred to above.[1]) If growth were kept down to the possible rate with a reserve of non-employed labour, the system could hardly be said to be in a state of internal equilibrium. The firms would always be straining to do more investment than they can. Any chance relaxation of credit would set them first increasing the stock of basic plant and then eating into the margin of non-employment, thus starting an inflation which would then be jerked to a halt. A golden age restrained by financial control, therefore, cannot be credited with short-period stability.

There is another way in which the desire to accumulate may be checked. When the scarcity of labour sets in, if the firms are under the influence of the fellow-feeling described by Adam Smith, they refrain from bidding up wage rates and trying to entice workers from each other. Each then has its own share of the labour force. If they realise the situation, they refrain from building plants that they will be unable to man. The desired rate of accumulation is then tailored to fit the possible rate. Or it may happen that each has built up productive capacity in the hope of getting hands, and, on the average, productive capacity is under-utilised. This situation may be kept alive by continual changes of fortune, each firm from time to time being lucky enough to get the labour it requires. The under-utilisation of plant reduces the rate of profit on capital. Overall steady growth would be established when the rate of profit expected (on the basis of average experience) is such that the rate of accumulation that it induces is brought down to the possible rate. In this case also short-period stability can hardly be supposed to prevail.

The type of restraint which is in force may be supposed to react upon the choice of technique. When the restraint operates simply by keeping the rate of interest at a level which dampens the desire to grow, there is no reason why the choice of technique

[1] P. 43.

should not be that appropriate to the ruling rate of profit. When the restraint operates by rationing of credit, firms may aim at less mechanised techniques than they would choose if they were untrammelled, though this will tend to increase the overall scarcity of labour and cause under-capacity working for lack of hands. When the restraint operates through monopsony in the labour market (so that each firm has its own group of workers and does not attempt to recruit any more) the techniques chosen are likely to be more mechanised than that which would maximise profits, and the rate of profit on capital is pushed down to such a level as to reduce the desired rate of growth to fit the actual rate that is being realised.

A Galloping Platinum Age

So far, we have considered situations in which the composition of the stock of capital is already adjusted to the rate of growth that is going on, so that the ratio of plant for producing plant to plant for producing commodities is such that it can maintain itself. Such a stock of capital does not drop from heaven. It has to be built up by a process of accumulation. We now examine the manner in which this process might develop.[1]

Let us suppose that 'animal spirits' are high, and a large mass of non-employed labour is available, but the desired rate of growth cannot be attained because of lack of basic plant to produce plant. The investment industries are experiencing a seller's market and a large part of investment is devoted to enlarging the investment sector ; as it grows, more labour is employed and the ratio of gross investment to the output of commodities rises as the process goes on. Consequently the rate of profits is rising. Unless technical progress is sufficiently rapid, the real-wage rate is falling.

In so far as the rate of profit has an influence upon the choice of technique, less mechanised methods of production are chosen at each round of gross investment, which causes employment to increase all the faster. If this gallop is not interrupted either by reaching full employment or striking the

---

[1] Ian Little ('Classical Growth', *Oxford Economic Papers*, June 1957) used the expression 'platinum age' for what we call, below, a 'creeping platinum age', in which the rate of accumulation is decelerating. It is convenient to use his metal also for an accelerating process.

minimum acceptable real-wage rate, it proceeds until the stock of basic plants has been brought to the ratio to consumption-sector plants appropriate to the desired rate of accumulation.

A Creeping Platinum Age

The reverse situation, in which the ratio of basic plant is too high for the physically possible rate of growth, does not appear to be a plausible one, but it has some scholastic interest.

To simplify the argument, let us suppose that there are no new inventions and discoveries, so that techniques are changed only by way of adaptation to changes in profits and wages. When the story begins full employment has already been reached, the rate of accumulation is at a peak, the rate of profit is high and techniques of a low degree of mechanisation are being installed. The labour force is not growing fast enough to keep up with employment offered by the growing stock of plant. To check the scarcity of labour that threatens, the rate of interest is raised and a brake is imposed upon accumulation ; the consequent fall in the rate of profit brings the desired rate of accumulation down. Labour is released from investment and becomes available to the commodity sector. A sufficiently skilful operation of the financial machine may be conceived to raise the rate of interest in such a way as to bring down the rate of accumulation gradually without causing unemployment. At each moment, then, the narrowing gap between the rate of profit and the rate of interest is just sufficient to call forth a rate of investment, which, together with the demand for commodities that it generates, just absorbs the whole labour force. As the rate of profit falls, more mechanised techniques are chosen at each round of investment.

The process continues until the rate of accumulation has come down approximately to equality with the rate of growth of the labour force. The stock of capital is then gradually adjusted to the technique appropriate to the rate of profit corresponding to that rate of accumulation.

Thus the path which the model follows resembles the path through logical time of an equilibrium model with a decelerating rate of accumulation, falling rate of profit, falling marginal efficiency of investment and rising real-wage rate, approaching asymptotically to a stationary state. There is an important difference, however. Our model is never exactly in equilibrium at any point on its path, for the technique of production chosen at each round of investment is that appropriate to the rate of profit expected on the basis of a projection of current prices, whereas in the equilibrium model techniques are chosen in the light of correct foresight of the movement of prices over the lifetime of each kind of capital good.[1]

A Bastard Golden Age

We must now consider another type of limit upon the rate of accumulation. Inflationary pressure, bringing financial checks into operation, may arise when there is no scarcity of labour—indeed a great mass of non-employment—if the real-wage rate refuses to be depressed below a particular level. A higher rate of accumulation means a lower real-wage rate. When the desired rate of accumulation is greater than the rate which is associated with the minimum acceptable real wage, the desire must be checked. A situation in which the rate of accumulation is being held in check by the threat of rising money wages due to a rise in prices (as opposed to rising money wages due to a scarcity of labour) may be described as a bastard golden age.[2]

The rate of accumulation may be less or greater than the rate of growth of population, so that non-employment is increasing or diminishing. (In the latter case the system is heading towards a legitimate golden age.)

A bastard golden age sets in at a fairly high level of real wages when organised labour has the power to oppose any fall in the real-wage rate. Any attempt to increase the rate of accumulation, unless it is accompanied by a sufficient reduction in consumption out of profits, is then frustrated by an inflation-

[1] Those who make pseudo-causal models to simulate the equilibrium path are somewhat casual in specifying the mechanism that produces the required result. For instance, Meade (*A Neo-classical Theory of Economic Growth*, p. 3.) merely postulates that monetary policy keeps the prices of consumption goods constant, while money-wage rates are such as to ensure full employment. He dodges the problem of foresight by making capital goods perfectly versatile. In his story the rate of interest *falls* with the rate of profit.

[2] Cf.R. F. Kahn, 'Exercises in the Analysis of Growth', *Oxford Economic Papers*, June 1959.

ary rise in money-wage rates. In such a situation, the rate of accumulation is limited by the 'inflation barrier'.

A low-level bastard golden age is seen when the real-wage rate is at the minimum level tolerable. (A low-level bastard golden age might have the same standard of life as obtains in a leaden age, but the mechanism of the system is different. In a leaden age the slow rate of accumulation keeps the standard of life to the minimum ; in the bastard golden age the minimum standard of life sets a limit to the rate of accumulation.)

A Bastard Platinum Age

When technical progress is going on, the amount of labour required to produce the minimum acceptable real wage for a given team of men is gradually falling. Then a constant level of real wages is compatible with a rise in the ratio of gross investment to consumption. Thus acceleration of accumulation can take place without causing inflation.

Summary

In golden ages the initial conditions are appropriate to steady growth. In true and limping golden ages the actual realised growth rate is limited only by the desired rate. (In a true golden age, the possible rate coincides with the desired rate and near full employment has already been reached.) In a restrained golden age, the realised growth rate is limited by the possible rate, and kept down to it. In a leaden age the possible rate is held down by the realised rate. In a bastard golden age the possible rate is limited in a different way—that is, by real wages being at the tolerable minimum. Both in a limping golden age and a bastard golden age the stock of capital in existence at any moment is less than sufficient to offer employment to all available labour. In the limping golden age the stock of equipment is not growing faster for lack of 'animal spirits'. In the bastard age it is not growing faster because it is blocked by the inflation barrier.

In platinum ages the initial conditions do not permit steady growth and the rate of accumulation is accelerating or decelerating as the case may be.

THE ROLE OF THRIFTINESS

We must now consider the effect of greater or less thriftiness upon the way these various processes develop.

Even in a situation of scarcity of labour a sharp, unforeseen rise of thriftiness — that is, a fall in expenditure on commodities — is liable to cause slumpy conditions, for the resources released from one type of production cannot immediately be transferred to another, and meanwhile profitability is reduced. For the moment we are not interested in such shock effects. We must therefore conduct our argument in terms of thriftiness *being* higher or lower, rather than rising or falling.

Golden Ages

With any particular rate of accumulation, higher thriftiness entails a lower rate of profit (and, at any stage of technical development, a higher level of real wages). It is therefore associated with a lower desired rate of accumulation. (This is shown on the diagram by the A curve lying lower, so that D lies further to the left on the I curve.) When the actual rate of growth is limited only by the desired rate, therefore, greater thrift is associated with a lower rate of accumulation. This is the central paradox of the *General Theory* projected into long-period analysis.

In a situation that would give rise to a true golden age at a particular level of thriftiness, a higher level causes the golden age to develop a limp. A lower level of thriftiness (by raising the rate of profit) would generate excess demand for labour and require the golden age to be put under restraint.

According to this way of looking at things, higher thriftiness cannot directly promote a higher rate of growth, but when the propensity to accumulate is higher than technical conditions allow to be realised, thriftiness tends to reduce the need for restraint and permits the possible growth to be realised at a higher level of real wages.

There is, however, a somewhat more subtle point involved if we allow for the effect of a high propensity to accumulate in speeding up the possible rate itself through induced innovations.

A Model of Accumulation

The restraints necessary to prevent a scarcity of labour from breaking out into inflation cannot be supposed to be just right ; to work at all, they are somewhat overdone ; they create and maintain a margin of unemployment. Thus, paradoxically, an excess demand for labour may be said to cause unemployment. The existence of a reserve of labour takes some of the steam out of the pressure for induced innovations ; moreover the restraints may be operated in a way that dampens 'animal spirits' all round by creating instability and therefore uncertainty.[1] Thus not only is the rate of accumulation held below the desired rate, but also the pace of technical progress is less than it would be if no restraints were imposed.

Now, with any particular total of equipment in existence, given the rate of accumulation being carried out, lower thriftiness entails a higher demand for labour. By creating a situation that calls restraints into operation, lower thriftiness may tend to reduce the rate of growth of the economy.

The connection between thrift and accumulation may also run partly in the inverse sense. A high propensity to accumulate may have some effect in making thriftiness higher, in so far as it causes firms to distribute less to rentiers in order to finance investment from their own net profits. (Similarly, in the age of private business of the Marshallian type, or in a peasant economy, investment opportunities are a direct cause of saving.)

It is a necessary condition for a golden age that effective demand should grow at the growth rate of the economy. When technical progress (which we assume to be neutral) is raising output per head, the real-wage rate must be rising equally, so that demand for commodities keeps step with output. This entails that competition between firms is strong enough to keep prices falling, relatively to money-wage rates, in step with costs. When monopolistic policies make prices sticky in face of falling costs (or when rises in money-wage rates are offset by raising prices in excess of the rise in costs) the *share* of profit, and therefore of saving, in income rises, but only because employment and output from given equipment is reduced. In such a case there is a fall in real wages (or a failure of the required rise)

[1] Cf. pp. 66-7.

61

without a corresponding increase in profits. (This matter is further discussed below.)

Platinum Ages

At each point in an accelerating or decelerating process of accumulation, the real wage corresponding to a given rate of accumulation is lower, the greater the proportion of profits consumed. The most important consequence of this is that low thriftiness may cause an acceleration process to be checked, by striking the minimum tolerable level of real wages, which with greater thriftiness would have been able to go further.

In a case where this limit is not encountered, we might imagine a complete history,[1] starting from a situation with a small amount of basic plant, much non-employment, and a high desired rate of growth galloping (with accelerating accumulation) until full employment is reached, then being checked and creeping (with decelerating accumulation) towards a golden-age path. Comparing the story for two economies alike except that one is more thrifty than the other (that is, with a higher proportion of saving to profits): in the more thrifty economy, Aleph, the real-wage rate is higher at each point in the story than in the less thrifty Beth. More mechanised techniques are chosen in Aleph and consequently the non-employed labour is absorbed more slowly. At the turning point when full employment is reached, the rate of output of commodities and (in a rough-and-ready sense) the stock of capital equipment, are greater in Aleph than they were at the corresponding turning point in Beth. The latest equipment installed in Aleph, before deceleration sets in, is of a degree of mechanisation that Beth will use only after having crept some way down the slope of the falling rate of profits.[2] Similarly, when each has come down to the permanently maintainable golden-age rate of accumulation, Aleph settles into it with a higher rate of output of com-

---

[1] We imagine it for the sake of exercising the model. It does not seem to have any particular relevance to reality, except as a warning against an unnecessarily onerous way of carrying out a plan of industrialisation.

[2] It is not possible, without filling in details about the character of the book of blue-prints which the two economies have in common, to make an exact comparison between them, for their respective histories have left each with a different selection of obsolescent equipment.

modities and a higher degree of mechanisation of technique. In this rather peculiar sense it is true to say that greater thriftiness promotes a greater accumulation of capital.

Bastard Ages

When it is the real wage (whether at a miserable or a comfortable level) which limits the rate of growth, greater thriftiness makes more investment possible in a perfectly straightforward and unambiguous sense. In that situation every scrap of consumption out of profits is directly at the expense of accumulation.

INSTABILITY

In order to keep the main line of long-run development clear we have assumed conditions of tranquillity in which unexpected events from without never occur and incompatibilities do not upset the system from within. We must now turn to the effect on accumulation of such chance changes.

Reaction to Shocks

We place the argument in the setting of a near-enough golden age with only a slight limp, that is to say that, in a broad sense, over the long run, steady accumulation is going on, and the average ratio of unemployed to employed labour is appreciable but not very large. There is a definite desired rate of accumulation ; a faster rate of accumulation would require a higher rate of profit than it would generate, and so cannot be sustained (the curves cut as shown at *D* in the diagram). Chance events, say a burst of consumer spending or an exceptionally attractive bout of innovations, from time to time raise effective demand and cause the level of profits to rise. And contrariwise.

We first examine the behaviour of the model when we retain the assumption that the prospective rate of profit on investment is calculated on the basis of today's prices.

On this assumption, the desired rate of growth is jerked upward by a change favourable to profits. (In the diagram the *A* curve is raised temporarily, moving *D* to the right.) While it is high, investment plans are laid for a faster rate of accumulation.

A raised level of profits may survive for a time after the initial cause of the movement has disappeared. This happens because many firms are making outlays on investment that will cause the stock of capital equipment in use to grow at faster than the former rate, when they are completed, but meanwhile the outlays of each firm are generating profits for all and none is taking into account the competition that it will have to meet when the plans of the others are completed. For a time, therefore, the level of profit remains high, suspended by its own bootstraps. As the new equipment emerges, productive capacity rises relatively to effective demand. The expectation of profit (projected from the current situation) deteriorates. Unless the drop is very severe, plans in the pipeline of production will be completed, but plans for further investment now fall below the level appropriate to the long-run desired rate of growth. After a time the level of profits drops below that appropriate to the long-run desired rate of accumulation. It is not so low, however, as to justify the fall in the rate of accumulation that has occurred (below *D*, the *A* curve lies above the *I* curve). 'Animal spirits' reassert themselves and a revival sets in, that carries the system, perhaps, a little beyond the long-run desired rate, so that another relapse follows, but the wobbles around the desired rate grow less, and near-enough stability is realised unless a fresh disturbance intervenes.[1]

The story can be told symmetrically for a downward movement starting from a chance fall in the level of profits ; a period of abnormally low gross investment is followed by a recovery temporarily beyond the desired rate of accumulation.

Over the course of fluctuations in the rate of accumulation, the production of commodities responds to the swings in gross investment, but the movements are much less than proportionate. If conditions of perfect competition prevailed in the

[1] This conception resembles Kalecki's trade-cycle model in which damped fluctuations are set going by random shocks. It differs from his in that the central point around which the cycles cycle is a rate of accumulation, not a stock of capital. In most discussions of fluctuations, the model is somehow suspended in the air without any indication of what causes it to be moving around one point rather than another. Kalecki's latest treatment of the subject ('Observations on the Theory of Growth', *Economic Journal*, March 1962) is formally the same as the above, but he makes technical progress an element in the desired, not in the possible, rate of growth.

commodity markets, plants in that sector would always be operated at capacity if they are operated at all, prices swinging up or down, relatively to money-wage rates, to equate demand to short-period supply (lowering and raising the level of real wages) so that scarcely any swings in production would occur. In reality, of course, markets for manufacturers are highly imperfect, prices are fairly sticky and changes in investment are generally accompanied by changes in output and employment in the commodity sector. Moreover, a higher level of profits in any one year leads to a rise in distribution to rentiers, and a rise in rentier receipts to a rise in their expenditure, which is spread over a considerable subsequent period. Thus the upswing in the rate of expenditure on commodities would be less than proportional to the rise in investment that caused them, even if there were no change in real-wage rates at all.

So far as rentier consumption is concerned, this lag in the reaction of changes in expenditure to changes in receipts may be supposed to be much more marked of a downswing than an upswing — an unforeseen fall in receipts reduces a household's saving rather than the standard of comfort to which they are accustomed. If incomes rose and remained at a steady level thereafter, we should expect expenditure to be restored to its normal proportion after a year or two, but if incomes fell and remained steady thereafter, the normal proportion might not be restored before a change-over of generations had occurred within the rentier families.

When we are concerned not with once-for-all changes but with fluctuations around a generally rising trend (as in a near-enough golden age in which technical progress is going on) this difference in reaction-time produces a ratchet effect, so that the low point of rentier expenditure is higher in each recession than the last, more or less in proportion to the rise in rentier income that has occurred meanwhile.

The lag in expenditure from profits combines with whatever effect there may be of changing prices (raising real-wage rates in a downswing and reducing them in an upswing) to make movements of overall output much less marked than of gross investment. (We generally think of the short-period multiplier as not much more than 2, arising from a marginal propensity to save

65

of 0·5, when the longrun proportion of investment to net income may be around 0·1.)

Where random fluctuations are known from experience to be liable to occur, it would be absurd to apply very strictly the assumption that firms revise their plans from day to day on the basis of today's receipts. We must suppose that a change in profits is of a certain magnitude or endures for a certain time before it leads to a revision of investment decisions. Since (for the reasons just given) fluctuations are sharper in investment-sector industries than in the commodity sector, they must be supposed to have a higher threshold of reaction. They have grown accustomed to an uneven load of demand; for them normal capacity operation is much less than physical full capacity (imperfect markets permit them to keep profit margins at a level that gives them a rate of profit on capital not less than is obtainable elsewhere).

This has an important bearing on the scale of the fluctuations set up by chance events. A small swing is met by an increase in investment which carries the basic industries nearer to full-capacity operation, without causing them to step up their own rate of accumulation. An upswing which carries through, so to say, to the second stage and deludes the basic industries into enlarging themselves faster than at the long-run desired rate, both causes a stronger and longer boom and leaves behind a longer period of sub-average profits and slower accumulation.

An economy which has been living through fluctuations in its rate of growth will have, at any moment, a stock of capital goods whose age-composition and division between sectors are not appropriate to steady growth; this in itself generates wobbles in development in the manner discussed above.

The underlying characteristics of a near-enough golden age may thus be overlaid with great variations in year-to-year experience.

Unsteady Control

The type of instability which we have been discussing so far arises from expectations based on projection of the present, chance events, and the time lags which permit a movement to be amplified before it becomes clear that it was inappropriate in the first place. The fluctuations run around a desired rate of accumulation which, in perfectly tranquil conditions, would be steadily maintained.

A restrained golden age, which is in any case constantly knocking its head against some barrier that prevents the desired rate of growth from being realised, would have greater stability if the restraint operated in a steady way. On the other hand, when it works by periodically penalising investment, causing unemployment, and then allowing it to be absorbed again, fluctuations are produced by the very operation of the restraint itself.[1]

Inherent Instability

A more radical kind of instability is seen when expectations are influenced by a projection, not just of today's situation, but of the movement experienced in the recent past, so that a rise in the level of profits sets up an expectation of a further rise, and a fall, of a further fall. (This may be taken to mean that when gross profit per plant has been rising it is expected to rise further ; or merely that an upward trend in receipts improves confidence and reduces the risk premium in the calculation of expected profits.)

We now adapt the model to expectations of this kind. When the rate of profit on investment, calculated on the basis of present prices and costs, has been rising, the desired rate of accumulation is higher, and when it has been falling, lower, than would correspond to the present rate of profit if it had been constant for some time.

In these conditions the firms are unable to settle down to a steady rate of accumulation. While the rate of profit is rising, the desired rate of accumulation is kept high, but as soon as the desired rate is reached, profits cease to rise, and that rate is no longer desired. Uncertainty, through the volatility of expectations to which it gives rise, is continually leading the firms into self-contradictory policies. Now it needs no chance shocks to set an upswing going. The model is inherently unstable and fluctuates even in otherwise tranquil conditions.

[1] This resembles Kalecki's political trade cycle. 'Political Aspects of Full Employment', *Political Quarterly*, October-December 1943.

Provided we do not put too much weight upon it, we can still make use of the diagram which maps possible short-period situations. When profits have been rising, the I curve (which indicates the rate of accumulation that the firms desire to carry out at the present rate of profit) has shifted to the right in the more or less recent past and the firms now find themselves carrying out too low a rate of accumulation to be satisfied. The rate will be higher in the near future.

When the rate of profit has recently ceased to rise or has been falling, the I curve has shifted to the left in the more or less recent past and the firms now find themselves with a ratio of basic to commodity-sector plant which is inappropriately high. A recession has already begun or is on the way.

The extent of fluctuations of this kind does not depend merely upon time lags; it depends upon the reaction of expectations to experience, and of investment plans to expectations. The self-magnifying boost due to an initial rise in the level of profits may be sufficiently strong to keep the upswing going after the greater rate of output of equipment emerging from the pipeline of production has begun to appear. To check a decline in investment plans, it is not sufficient for the rate of accumulation to be abnormally low — it must have ceased to fall.

There is an important difference between the upward and the downward phases of the oscillations which the economy experiences. An upswing, however much momentum it develops, cannot continue indefinitely, for if it does not bring itself to a halt first, it will run up against the limit set by the availability of labour and bring the anti-inflationary restraints into operation. There is no such limit on the downward tack. (Even total cessation of activity in the investment sector is not a limit, for then disinvestment of working capital in the commodity sector could set in.) Relief comes from another quarter.

As we have seen, a fall in expenditure lags behind a fall in income. As income falls, expenditure rises as a proportion of income (the ratio of saving to consumption falls). Consequently the gross profit corresponding to a given level of investment-sector employment rises as the level of profits falls. At some

68

point gross profits cease to fall with falling investment and at this point the run down ceases.[1]   According to our assumptions, when the fall comes to an end, the desire to accumulate springs up again, and so the rate of profit rises.

With expectations which react in this way, the rate of accumulation is never steady, nor does it fall into a regular cycle (if it did so, its movements would become predictable and the uncertainty that caused them would disappear) ; investment takes place in a series of rushes, each of which leaves behind traces which affect the conditions in which the next will occur.

Unsteady Growth

Superimposing inherent instability upon the chance changes analysed above, we see the model in a perpetual state of perturbation.   At any moment the stock of capital embodies the consequences of misguided investments made in the past ; its age-composition is all higgledy-piggledy, and its division between sectors is never exactly appropriate to the investment now being planned.

All the same, in a broad way, our analysis of long-run growth remains cogent.   True, it cannot be discussed in terms of *the* desired rate of accumulation, for at each moment some different rate of growth is being planned.   But the range of rates of growth (experienced over the course of fluctuations) tends to have a higher average when 'animal spirits' are high and thriftiness low.   The propensity to accumulate may be high relative to the physically possible rate of growth, so that booms generally run into scarcity of labour and have to be restrained, or it may be low so that unemployment persists even during the peaks of activity, and, perhaps, grows from boom to boom.   The proportion of investment to consumption may be growing or falling from boom to boom.   Thus the characteristic features of restrained and limping golden ages or of platinum ages can be discerned under the restless surface of unstable growth.

[1] In the language of accepted trade-cycle theory, the upswing may be halted when the accelerator ceases to accelerate ; the downswing, when the multiplier ceases to multiply.

WAGES AND PRICES

In our model, as in reality, the level of money-wage rates obtaining at any particular moment is an historical accident. The absolute level of wages in terms of money affects nothing except the words and numbers in which money values are reckoned and the nominal value of the stock of currency. But changes in the level of money-wage rates have important effects upon the behaviour of the economy in real terms.

The causes of movements in money-wage rates are bound up with the competition of different groups of workers to maintain or improve their relative positions, and the consequences of changes in wage levels are most important in connection with the competition in international trade. Our highly aggregated model is therefore ill suited to discussing them ; only some very general remarks can be made within its framework.

We have found three kinds of situation in which money-wage rates are bound to rise. The first is where there is a scarcity of labour in the sense that firms possess or are in the course of building more plant than they can man for capacity operation, when they expect to be able to sell capacity output at profitable prices, and they are not inhibited by monopsonistic solidarity amongst themselves from bidding for labour.

The second case arises in an economy where organised labour refuses to submit to any fall in the level of real wages below what they have once obtained. There, any rise in the price of commodities normally purchased by workers, relatively to the level of money wages, sets up an irresistible demand for a rise in money-wage rates. This is what we have called a high-level bastard golden age.

The third case is seen in a low-level bastard golden age where real wages are at the subsistence minimum, so that any rise in the price of food-stuffs (due, say, to a harvest failure), or any attempt to increase the rate of accumulation, forces employers to offer higher money-wage rates in order to enable their workers to live.

Quite apart from these cases, the level of money-wage rates may be continuously rising simply because it is easier for each group of employers to give way to the demands of their workers and recoup themselves by raising prices than to incur the losses and unpleasantness involved in resisting them.

In a golden age (with no saving out of wages) the rate of profit on capital is determined by the rate of growth and the proportion of profits consumed. Gross profit margins, that is, the ratio of prices to prime costs, must then be such as to yield a profit per man employed that yields profit at the given rate upon the value of capital per man in each line of production.

To maintain a constant level of prices for commodities requires that the overall rate of rise of hourly money-wage rates is just equal to the overall rate of rise of output per man-hour. This could only be the result of a happy fluke.

When money-wage rates rise at a faster pace, prime costs in money terms are rising. The reaction of firms to changing prime costs may be very various. We consider only the simplest case. We assume that the mark-up on prime costs (Kalecki's 'degree of monopoly') is established by a convention which is maintained when prime costs rise. Thus, as money-wage rates rise, the firms raise prices, with no time lag, in proportion to their prime costs. Real-wage rates, therefore, are the same as they would be at constant prices.

Payments to rentiers are related to profits of some time ago. The real income of rentiers is therefore lower when prices are rising with prime costs than when they are constant. The effect is the same as that which would be brought about (at constant prices) by a correspondingly lower distribution of interest and dividends by the firms.[1] In so far as rentiers react simply to the current real purchasing power of their receipts, their consumption in real terms is less. The effect is similar to that brought about by higher thriftiness. Now, if the conventional gross profit margin was compatible with normal capacity operation of plant at constant prices, it causes under-utilisation of plant in the commodity sector when prices have been raised relatively to total money incomes. The rate of profit on capital

---

[1] Other classes of incomes which are affected by changing prices — salaries, social security benefits, rents for real estate etc. — have been excluded from our model. There are many important consequences of inflation which we therefore do not discuss.

(calculated on the basis of today's prices and costs) is therefore lower.

There is another way in which rising wages may tend to have a deleterious effect on profits. From the point of view of firms taken as a whole, receipts are rising at the same pace as the purchasing power of money, over commodities and labour, is falling. For the firms collectively, therefore, current amortisation quotas cover current replacements of equipment. But, for any one firm, when a replacement of capital equipment falls due, the cost of the corresponding new plant exceeds the amortisation quotas accumulated over its life, since it has lived through a period when gross profits in money terms were lower than corresponds to the costs ruling today. Thus (apart from the bonus due to lower real distribution to rentiers), the firms have to do more outside borrowing to maintain a given rate of accumulation when money-wage rates are rising. This might tend to have a discouraging effect on accumulation.

These depressing influences, however, are a very light weight to set against the highly stimulating effect of an *expectation* of rising prices and wages. When rentiers are expecting that the prices of commodities will be higher in the future, the proportion of expenditure (especially on durable goods) to current receipts is stepped up, so that thriftiness in real terms is lower. When the firms are expecting that wages will be higher in the future, they hurry forward their investment plans. Thus once an inflationary process has set in, it raises the rate of profit and so pours oil on its own fire.

Text-book analysis is often conducted on the basis of something called 'money' without which transactions cannot be carried out. When the stock of 'money' is fixed, a rise in money-wage rates and prices which increases the nominal value of transactions at any given real level of output causes the rate of interest to rise so as to speed up the velocity of circulation of 'money'. But a rise in the rate of interest reduces real output, by restraining investment. Thus a rise in money-wage rates is a direct cause of unemployment.

All this seems rather a tall story. In our model there is no such automatic mechanism, but there are authorities who take a view about the general level of prices and use control over the supply of bank credit as a means to check what they consider an undesirable rise. If they exercise this control, not only when the rate of accumulation that the firms want to carry out is straining at the limits of the possible rate, but whenever prices are rising, they are liable to set a serious drag upon accumulation.[1]

Now consider the situation when money-wage rates rise less, on the average, than output per head; prime costs are then falling. If the firms cut prices proportionately, the real-wage rate and the real income of rentiers would evolve in exactly the same way as if money-wage rates rose in proportion to output per head and prices were constant.[2] But it is unnatural to assume that firms are as keen to cut prices when costs fall as to raise them when costs rise.

When prices and wage rates are both sticky, we should expect to see a concertina effect on profit margins. When costs fall, as a result of rising output per head, while prices are kept more or less constant, demand fails to expand with productivity. With gradually increasing profit margins, output increases less than output per head, and unemployment and under-utilisation of equipment grow. Consequently investment is discouraged and the rate of accumulation falls. The firms are cutting off their nose to spite their face, and higher profit margins are leading to lower profits. At some point the stickiness of prices breaks down in one market after another, and a burst of competition brings profit margins down with a run. Output now expands. An armistice is declared in the price wars; a new price level becomes established and the whole process starts over again. There is no guarantee, however, that the reduction of margins in the competitive phases fully compensates for the rises that take place in between, so that there may be an upward drift in margins over the long run.

Fortunately, periods of continuously falling money-wage rates are not a common experience, but, for the sake of symmetry, we may consider the case of falling money-wage rates accompanied by a fall in prices proportional to prime costs. By analogy with the case of rising prices discussed above, we

---

[1] Cf. above p. 67, note.
[2] Cf. p. 97.

see that the real income of rentiers is higher than with constant prices and the rate of profit higher. The rising purchasing power of gross profits retained from earlier periods tends to encourage net investment. But, swamping these encouraging influences, an expectation of falling prices and wages strongly discourages both expenditure[1] and investment, and so reduces the rate of accumulation.

These various effects of changes in money-wage rates play across the various real movements discussed above. This makes the operation of the model complicated and confusing. That, however, is a merit, not a defect, since it corresponds to reality.

NATURAL RESOURCES

There is a sort of hubris in setting up a model in which all output is produced by human labour with the aid of man-made equipment, forgetting the kindly fruits of the earth. The foregoing model cannot be applied, even in the broadest way, to actual problems until it has been supplemented by an analysis of the supplies of natural resources available to the economy. There is not much to be said about it, however, at the very high level of generality of the foregoing argument, since, just because they are natural, natural resources cannot be aggregated. Here we only mention, by way of warning, some of the complications that must be introduced into the model, without attempting to develop them.[2]

Prices

The pattern of equilibrium prices includes some elements governed by supply and demand. When competition prevails

---

[1] There is no room in our model for the so-called 'Pigou effect' because there is no form of property except the obligations of firms or banks. Where there is a national debt (including the note issue), its holders find their real wealth rising when prices fall, while the debtors, that is the taxpayers, do not react to the corresponding increase in the real burden that they are bearing. Thus, there may be a reduction in thriftiness and a consequent increase in employment. (The economists who are fond of deploying this somewhat far-fetched argument in favour of cutting wages have a strange propensity to confuse falling prices with low prices.)

[2] The inclusion of land in the formal argument is attempted in my *Accumulation of Capital*, Book VI.

and there is a uniform rate of profit on capital throughout the whole economy, we can make use of Marshall's device of 'cost at the margin' for each kind of animal, vegetable or mineral product. But, when there is not a free flow of investment between manufacturers and primary production, the argument has to be conducted in terms of the analysis of trade between the sectors of the economy.

Fluctuations

Industries which are highly competitive and have short-period conditions of supply that are very inelastic, experience great swings of prices with even small fluctuations in the overall level of effective demand. Primary production generally has this characteristic. In addition, being geographically concentrated, the incomes of whole communities fluctuate dramatically with the prices of particular products.

Disturbances

Agricultural production is subject to natural disasters and the vagaries of the weather so that output varies erratically, introducing disturbances into the rest of the economy.

Disproportionalities

As the whole economy develops, most demands expand, and some run into bottlenecks of limited supplies of natural resources. During a period of scarcity for a particular product its price is high and its producers prosperous. Users set about to find substitutes and alternative sources of supply may be opened up. Prices fall and prosperity comes to an end. The new sources of supply, though called into existence by high prices, once developed, are not necessarily high-cost producers; and in any case they are not easily forced out of existence again. In such cases, a short period in a seller's market leads to a long period in a buyer's market.

Politics

For these reasons the free play of market forces creates conditions that will not be tolerated by a community that has any power to control them.

A Golden Age

The conditions for a near-enough golden age, which do not seem very far-fetched when we consider the industrial sector of an economy alone, become extremely implausible when primary production is included in the picture. And even when, on a broad view, something not too far from a golden age is realised for a whole economy, it may conceal violent differences of fortune for particular communities within it.

INHERENT VICE

The conception of equilibrium in economic theory is a metaphor drawn from the relation between bodies in space. The balls come to rest in the bowl and when they are not disturbed they remain motionless. In time, there is no motionless rest. Time marches on. A stationary state, for instance, is not a state of passive inaction. It requires continuous purposive action to maintain a given physical stock of capital. It requires action to maintain the population. It requires action to maintain the level of skill and technical knowledge. To construct this 'famous fiction' we have to invent a balance of motives and restraints that cause it to be. All the more so when our fiction is not of continuous self-reproduction but of continuous smooth steady growth.

We have already noticed how money wages pursue a course of their own not tethered to the real development of the economy. There are a number of other loose elements in our model which are free to develop in their own way as time goes by ; they are liable to do so in a manner deleterious to the harmony of an otherwise near-enough golden age.

Economies of Scale

The direction of technical development may lead to an increase in the minimum efficient size of particular investments, and the general increase of production may be accompanied by an increase in specialisation (in the manufacture of components, etc.). Both tendencies increase the riskiness of investment for individual firms and so dampen 'animal spirits'.

A Model of Accumulation

The Size of Firms

Vigorous competition has a tendency to bring itself to an end by leaving a victor in possession of the field. As more and more markets come to be dominated by old-established, powerful firms, the fear of new competition grows less, and, with it, the urge to accumulate and to reduce costs is weakened. True, wars between giants may continue, but they cannot be relied upon to keep up the continuous pressure necessary for steady growth.

The ossifying effects of success operate also through the supply of finance. At any moment the bulk of profits is accruing to the older firms while the most lively would-be innovators have to borrow from outside and so find funds harder to come by.

Consumer Demand

With rising real income per household there may be a tendency for the overall propensity to consume to decline, in the sense that it requires more and more ingenuity and sales pressure to stimulate the jaded appetite of consumers and 'create wants' for even more goods. There may also be a low income-elasticity of demand for goods as opposed to services.[1] In so far as incomes earned in supplying services are spent on goods the manufacturing firms do not suffer from a failure of demand, but the growth of a somewhat rentier-minded professional class is liable to increase the overall thriftiness of the economy. Moreover, demand at a high standard of life is liable to be more fickle, which once more increases the riskiness of investment for the firms.

Profit Margins

Under a regime of oligopoly and price-leadership it is natural that the firms should show more alacrity in raising prices when money costs rise, than in lowering them when money costs fall, so that the varying relations between costs and prices described above are liable to lead, on balance, to an upward drift of profit margins, as time goes by. The consequent fall in the share of real wages in the value of output prevents demand (in real

[2] Cf. p. 18.

terms) per man employed from rising as fast as output per man. It is true that higher margins tend to be largely absorbed by higher selling costs, but the incomes derived from them (in advertising agencies, etc.) are likely to be of the middle-class type referred to above.

Stagnation

In all these ways, there is a tendency for a near-enough golden age to drift into a state of stagnation, with a falling growth rate, unless sufficiently strong favourable shocks occur from time to time to keep it running.

APPENDIX

A MODEL OF MODELS

Models of private-enterprise economies, in which the product of industry is distributed as wages and profits, can be grouped according to the mechanism which determines that distribution. In classical models, the real wage is fixed by the needs of the workers and profit is the residual surplus. In neo-classical models, the rate of interest is the supply price of capital and wages are the residual. In Keynesian models, the distribution of the product is governed by investment and thriftiness.

Classical Models

The classical model is most at its ease when there is a single wage good, 'corn', and the wage is agreed and paid in terms of it. It is a great simplification (though not essential to the argument[1]) if we further assume that no capital goods except seed corn are required to produce corn. There is an indefinite amount of labour available at a given corn-wage rate.

Capitalists receive their share in kind and can do what they like with it. They can eat it, or use it to employ workers to produce goods and services for them ; they can invest it in

[1] See P. Sraffa, *The Production of Commodities by Means of Commodities*, §§ 1-6.

78

increasing corn-producing capacity by providing seed and paying more workers to prepare for a larger output for the next period ; or they can let it rot.

What they do with their corn has no effect upon the rate of profit. But the rate at which they are investing corn in causing the production of corn to increase governs the rate of increase of the total labour force employed by them.

When capitalists use all their corn for investment in corn-production (consuming none themselves, and using none to employ workers to provide goods and services for them), the rate of profit is equal to the rate of accumulation, which is then the highest that is physically possible.

This model was suited to its original purpose—the analysis of diminishing returns from land and the division of the surplus between profit and rent. When we try to go further in elaborating an analysis of the accumulation of capital, we find that the corn wage has led us into a blind alley.

We can dispense with the assumption that there is only one wage good, provided that a specific physical quantity of each of a variety of commodities is required to support each size of family. The basket of wage goods then reproduces itself with a surplus, just as corn did, and the rest of the argument proceeds as before. (This is the basis of von Neumann's famous model.)

But now we come upon a serious difficulty. When employers specialise, some producing one kind of wage good and some another, a strictly non-monetary system is impossible. The wage must be agreed and the workers paid in terms of an acceptable medium of general purchasing power, whether one of the commodities or token money. (For each employer to pay with his own product, leaving the workers to deal, means that the economy is based on some kind of profit-sharing system, radically different from capitalism.[1])

When the wage is expressed in terms of money, the real wage emerges through the prices of commodities. The real wage may well be established at a minimum given by physical needs or social convention. But the condition that the real

---

[1] In my *Accumulation of Capital*, the assumption of a single composite consumption good is a mere simplification and does not have to take any weight ; the wage bargain is not made in terms of it.

wage has got to have, somehow or other, a certain value in terms of particular commodities, does not provide a mechanism for settling the relation between prices and costs. If one ingredient of the wage-basket, say salt, is produced by a monopolist, he may fix a price that yields him a higher rate of profit on his own capital than that which obtains in the economy as a whole. Then other sellers must accept a lower rate (paying money wages high enough to permit the workers to buy the necessary quantity of salt without letting the higher cost affect their own prices). If they are not willing to accept the position, there is an endless inflation of money wages and prices, and a growing scarcity of hands due to the real wage having fallen below the necessary supply price of labour.

To make the model workable, we might assume that the capitalists know the rate of profit that the economy as a whole enjoys, and charge prices on the basis of 'full costs' in such a way that each receives that rate of profit on his own capital. Or taking any set of prices that happened to be ruling (including some, perhaps, of a monopolistic character) we may suppose that the money wage was originally negotiated in terms of the 'cost of living' and that prices are rarely altered. But, either way, we are patching up the gap in the model rather awkwardly.

The conception of a wage bargain conducted in real terms is not only formally unacceptable but also seriously misleading. If real wages tended to rise when there is a scarcity of labour, we should see (as Marx expected to find) low real-wage rates per man-hour (not just low earnings) in a slump and high in a boom. This is contrary to experience where competitive conditions obtain. It is true that oligopolistically sticky prices may fail to fall, in a slump, when money wages are cut. But if so, the consequent fall in real wages causes an increase in unemployment, instead of a relief.

All the same, the corn-wage model is useful for working out the relationships that must obtain (as opposed to the mechanism through which they are established) when the level of real wages cannot be allowed to fall (whether because it is at the physical minimum or for any other reason).

Moreover, the model is indispensable for the analysis of planned industrialisation of a backward over-populated country.

Appendix

In such a situation the maximum rate of accumulation possible is set by the rate of growth of the output of wage-goods. The authorities must take a view of what the level of real wages should be, and they must see to it that money prices in relation to money-wage rates are such as to implement their decisions. In short, they have to make the actual economy, as best they may, approximate to the classical model.

Neo-Classical Models

The neo-classical model is most at its ease in a stationary state. The amount of capital that capitalists are willing to maintain in being (neither saving nor dissaving) is a function of the rate of interest or, alternatively, there is one rate of interest at which net saving is zero. The physical stock of capital and the real-wage rate are such as to have brought the rate of profit into equality with the rate of interest. There is then one value of the stock of capital that yields the rate of return (with a given labour force fully employed) which will cause it to be maintained. This is the value of capital that satisfies the conditions of the stationary state.

When it leaves the stationary state, the neo-classical model is all at sea. With any given value of capital in existence, the amount of saving that the capitalists wish to do to increase it depends upon the rate of interest, which must be equal to the rate of profit, but how can we tell what the rate of profit is till we know the rate of accumulation?

It is an illusion to suppose that 'the marginal productivity of capital' provides an independent determinant of the rate of profit. A 'quality of capital' in terms of value has no meaning in terms of physical productivity until the prices of its physical components are known, and this involves the rate of profit. A 'quantity of capital' in terms of a list of physical capital goods appropriate to various kinds of output, if they are taken to be fully utilised, entails the output of investment goods, and so the rate of accumulation, independently of the rate of profit that is supposed to determine it. If they are not necessarily fully utilised, then we have to know the current rate of investment to find out the state of effective demand and current profits. Whatever we do, we are one equation short.

The reason why the model works all right in the stationary state has nothing to do with its stationariness. It works because the rate of accumulation—zero—is specified. With any specified rate of accumulation, the function connecting saving with the rate of profit determines the position, for it shows what the rate of profit and the value of capital must be to make saving equal to investment at full employment.

The stationary state, in terms of our model, is the golden age appropriate to a zero growth rate. In the stationary state, the neo-classical model is holding the Keynesian model by the hand. When it lets go, it drifts off into indeterminacy.

There is a quite different refuge for the neo-classical model. This is in the non-monetary type of system described above.[1] In an economy of artisans, where every worker owns his own tools and finances his own production, there is no wage or rate of profit on capital. Each individual has an income from work and finance combined, depending on his physical production and its price in the market. Each has his own prospective return, in terms of future earnings over present consumption forgone, on savings invested in his own business. If all have the same rate of time preference (or if finance can be borrowed at a uniform rate of interest), each will cease to invest when the prospective rate of return on further investment has sunk to the same level. But then they will be in a stationary state. Until then each has his own prospective marginal return and the rate of profit on capital in the economy as a whole has no meaning.

A great part of neo-classical analysis is concerned with an economy of this kind, where prices are ruled by supply and demand and 'costs of production' consist of the individuals' subjective efforts and sacrifices.

The habit of hopping to and fro between this model and one in which costs of production are governed by a wage rate and rate of profit uniform throughout the economy, has been a plentiful source of confusion.

Keynesian Models

The Keynesian models (including our own) are designed to project into the long period the central thesis of the *General*

[1] See pp. 1-6.

Theory, that firms are free, within wide limits, to accumulate as they please, and that the rate of saving of the economy as a whole accommodates itself to the rate of investment that they decree.

It is unfortunate that this type of model has become associated with the formula $g = s/v$ (the rate of growth is equal to the proportion of income saved divided by the ratio of 'capital' to income).

When s is the *ex post* inverse ratio of net income to net investment (depending on the propensities to consume of various classes, the distribution of income between them, and the convention used for calculating depreciation in reducing gross to net income and investment) and v is the *de facto* ratio of the value of capital to the same net income (depending upon technical conditions and the level of utilisation of plant, as well as on the method of calculating depreciation and the value of plant) then the formula is a tautology of a particularly vapid character, as can be seen if we write it (for one unit of time) as :

$$\frac{\dot{K}}{K} = \frac{\dot{K}}{Y} \cdot \frac{Y}{K},$$

where K and Y are capital and income, in whatever units we please.

On the other hand, if s is somehow governed by an *ex ante* propensity to save of the economy as a whole and v is somehow determined by technical conditions, then the formula seems to be saying that firms are obliged to accumulate at the rate dictated by the propensity to save of the economy as a whole, which is quite contrary to the spirit of a Keynesian model.[1]

The Keynesian models can be classified according to the assumption made about the inducement to invest.

The capital-stock-adjustment mechanism.—Harrod,[2] the great

[1] Cf. p. 27.
[2] *Towards a Dynamic Economics*. The least difficult exposition of his model is 'Domar and Dynamic Economics', *Economic Journal*, September 1959. Domar, though often treated as Harrod's twin, does not propose any formula for the inducement to invest, and his model cannot properly be assigned to the Keynesian group. 'Expansion and Employment', *American Economic Review*, March 1947 and *Essays in the Theory of Economic Growth*.

pioneer in this field, relies upon the capital-stock-adjustment mechanism. Firms plan, for each period, an amount of investment calculated to bring the physical capacity of their plant to the level required to produce, at a normal level of utilisation of plant, the rate of output that they are actually producing today. That is to say, accumulation occurs under the influence of over-utilisation of plant.

Harrod gives two accounts of how this works out. The first is the instability principle. Starting in any particular situation, with whatever productive capacity there happens to be, a rise in the rate of investment, with the accompanying rise in consumption, governed by the multiplier, will cause the degree of over-utilisation of plant to increase, and so cause a further rise of investment to take place. And conversely for a fall.

In the other story there is, in any situation, a *warranted* rate of growth, which, if the firms happen to fall into it, will perpetuate itself so long as the *natural* rate of growth, compounded of the rate of increase of the labour force and of output per head (due to technical progress, which is assumed to be neutral) is great enough to permit it to run its course unchecked.

The existence of a warranted rate of growth means that the relationship between technical conditions, the propensity to consume and the eagerness of firms to achieve a normal degree of utilisation, is such that there is a particular degree of over-utilisation of plant which will cause such an amount of investment to be undertaken as will generate such a level of effective demand as will keep the stock of plant over-utilised to just that extent as it grows.

When the initial conditions are such that this degree of over-utilisation prevails (the required degree being greater the lower the marginal propensity to consume) and the age-composition of the stock of plant is such that a rate of gross investment growing at the warranted rate will reproduce those initial conditions from period to period, then the firms will carry out that gross investment and the warranted rate of growth will be realised. We are told that the firms will then be 'content with what they have done' as each scheme of investment is completed, but this evidently means that they will be discontented with the capacity which they now have to just the same extent (proportionately to the stock now in existence) as they were when that scheme of investment was planned.

Duesenberry [1] has elaborated this conception and shows that when conditions are such that there *is* a warranted rate of growth, it will be realised. He believes that a kindly providence arranged the technical and social conditions in the U.S.A. in the nineteenth century so as to produce a warranted rate of growth and to make it of the right magnitude to fit the natural rate of growth. [2] Harrod, on the other hand, believes that, even if there is a warranted rate of growth, and even if the economy does get into it sometimes, it is likely to be too high for the natural rate (because the propensity to consume is too low) and will never be enjoyed for long before it breaks its neck at full employment. In our terminology Duesenberry's system leads to a near-enough golden age, while Harrod's has occasional runs in a limping golden age with a falling ratio of non-employment.

Another approach is to use the capital-stock-adjustment mechanism to account for cyclical movements (either damped and kept alive by shocks or explosive and restrained by a ceiling) and to rely upon the natural rate of growth to introduce its own trend.

The trend may be introduced through the propensity to consume. [3] When the labour force is growing and output per head rising, a boom which raised output to the same level as was reached in the preceding boom would be accompanied by a larger amount of unemployment. The unemployed have some means of consumption which is not at the expense of any other consumption (say, deficit finance of a social insurance fund). Thus the ratio of consumption to investment in this boom is higher than in the last, and an upward trend in output is assured. This yields something like a limping golden age with a constant long-run average ratio of non-employment.

Alternatively, an element of Schumpeter's theory is brought into the story. [4] During the slack phase of a cycle, inventions and

---

[1] *Business Cycles and Economic Growth.*
[2] *Op. cit.*, p. 238.
[3] See R. C. O. Matthews, 'The Savings Function and the Problem of Trend and Cycle', *Review of Economic Studies*, 1954–55.
[4] See R. M. Goodwin, 'A Model of Cyclical Growth' in *The Business Cycle in the Post War-World* (ed. E. Lundberg).

discoveries remain unexploited and each boom finds an accumulation of investment opportunities which carry it up to full employment with a higher level of output than was reached last time. This one might expect to lead to irregular upward movements in ages sometimes of one metal and sometimes of another.

The desired capital/output ratio. In Kaldor's model[1] the inducement to invest is an increasing function of the rate of profit and a decreasing function of the ratio of the value of capital to the value of output (which is presumed to correspond to the physical rigidity, and therefore riskiness, of investment). At any given level of the rate of profit, the rate of accumulation that firms wish to carry out is a decreasing function of the capital/output ratio. Therefore, for any rate of accumulation there is one value of the capital/output ratio, which we may call the *desired* ratio, that is compatible with the firms being willing to sustain that rate of accumulation. Since full employment is assumed, this leads to the rather curious conclusion that the desired capital/output ratio is higher the faster the rate of growth of population.

When technical conditions and the initial stock of capital are such as to provide for full employment at the desired capital/output ratio, the economy grows under golden-age conditions. There is no problem corresponding to the conflict between the natural and the warranted rate of growth in the Harrod model, or to the relation of desired to possible accumulation in ours, for it is only in conditions of full employment that investment takes place at all (though it is by no means clear why this should be so).

Finance. Profit influences investment not only by providing the motive for it but also through providing the means. An important part of the gross investment of firms is financed by gross retained profits. Moreover, the amount that a firm puts up of its own finance influences the amount that it can borrow from outside.

---

[1] 'A Model of Economic Growth', *Economic Journal*, December 1957; and 'Economic Growth and the Problem of Inflation', Part I, *Economica*, August 1959. In a later version (not yet published, April 1962) a similar conclusion is drawn from different assumptions.

Appendix

Kalecki [1] makes investment plans for any period a function of the firms' gross savings of the immediate past period, and of the expected rate of profit. The gross savings are a proportion of the gross profit which was generated by the gross investment of that past period. Expected profits depend upon the gross investment of the current period and the stock of capital. Thus investment schemes, while they are being carried out, tend to encourage further investment to be planned, but when they emerge from the pipeline as additions to the stock of capital, they tend to discourage further investment.

This was the basis of his model of a 'pure' trade cycle [2] (which is the prototype of all the modern models). To introduce a trend, he relies upon a flow of inventions, each of which raises expected profits, and so stimulates investment. This seems rather a precarious source of a motive for accumulation; if continuous accumulation did result from it, in the manner of a golden age, the actual rate of profit would be constant.

Animal spirits.—In our model, the inducement to invest is conceived in terms of a desired rate of growth rather than a desired stock of capital. The natural rate of growth permits but does not cause actual growth. The actual trend of growth is generated from within by the propensity to accumulate inherent in the system. It is steady or fluctuating according as it operates in tranquil conditions which generate inertia, or in a chancy world where uncertainty makes expectations volatile.

Conclusion

These models are all too much simplified and too highly integrated for it to be possible to confront them with evidence from reality. At this stage, they must be judged on the *a priori* plausibility of their assumptions.

There is an important difference in emphasis between them according as they exhibit some kind of inbuilt propensity to maintain full employment over the long run or as they follow Keynes in regarding it as dependent upon enterprise that cannot be relied upon, unassisted, either to achieve stability in the short run or to maintain an adequate rate of growth in the long run.

[1] *The Theory of Economic Dynamics.*
[2] *Essays in the Theory of Economic Fluctuations.*

III

A MODEL OF TECHNICAL PROGRESS

THE analysis of an economy in which technical progress is going on cannot be made both neat and lifelike. There is nothing in reality which remains constant through time to provide us with neat units in which to calculate. Workers are acquiring new skills and losing old ones. Products are changing in physical character, in saleability and in capacity to satisfy wants. The wants themselves are changing with the products. The purchasing power of money over commodities, or over labour-time, or over both, is changing not only in general level but also in pattern. Above all, capital goods are changing, so that the means of production required for a later technique have little or nothing in common with those of earlier design. On the other hand, analysis which does not take account of technical change can be very neat but it is of no interest. The purpose of the present paper is to set up a highly simplified model in terms of which analysis can be conducted in a definite clear-cut manner, in the hope that it may yield insights that retain some validity when applied to the vaguer and more complicated processes of actual development.

THE MODEL

General Simplifying Assumptions

The argument is confined to a closed system of pure competitive private enterprise. As in the foregoing model, all production is organised in capitalist firms ; there are two classes of households—workers and rentiers ; total net income is exhaustively divided into wages and net profits ; there are no scarce factors of production and no economies of scale (beyond the efficient size of an individual plant) in any one line or for output as a whole.

A Model of Technical Progress

Special Assumptions

In order to reduce to a minimum the physical changes brought about by technical progress, we assume that the output of consumption goods is homogeneous and does not change, in specification or composition, as time goes by ; and we assume a constant, homogeneous labour force. Furthermore we assume that industry can be sharply divided into two sectors—one producing equipment and the other producing consumption goods. The whole of technical progress is concentrated on improving the design of equipment for use in the consumption-good sector. The *basic plant* required to equip the investment sector is used to produce itself and to produce the consumption-sector equipment. The specification of basic plant remains physically unchanged through time, each plant requiring an unchanging team of workers to operate it. Only its product is altering.

The physical specification of newly produced consumption-sector equipment is constantly changing, but we have provided ourselves with three units in which it can be measured—capacity output, employment offered, and real cost.

The physical cost of an outfit of equipment for the consumption-good sector consists in a certain amount of labour-time and basic-plant time ; when a given rate of profit is ruling uniformly throughout an economy there is a determinate pattern of normal prices (governed by costs of production including profit at the ruling rate on the capital involved) which can be expressed in terms of labour-time.[1] By the *real cost* of a piece of consumption-sector equipment we mean its price when new in terms of labour-time, at the ruling rate of profit.

For simplicity of exposition we take the money-wage rate constant and we take as the unit for consumption-sector equipment a *plant* employing a given number of men when operated at its normal capacity. Thus the money value of a plant is a measure of capital per head in the consumption-good sector, given the rate of profit, given the ratio of working to fixed capital when plant is working at capacity, and given the service life of plant.

[1] Cf. above, p. 10.

As a further simplification we assume that the number of firms, though large, is constant through time. Each firm can operate an indefinite number of plants without experiencing either economies or diseconomies of scale.

CLASSIFICATION

At any moment, there is in existence a pool of potential improvements, continually fed by new discoveries, from which firms are continually drawing new designs, each making the best it can devise at the moment. The new designs of each year are an improvement on those known up till then. Since we are not interested in the fortunes of particular firms, we will assume that each batch of new designs represents improvements all equivalent to each other.

Neutral, Biased and Partial Improvements

Our model provides a very simple criterion for classifying types of improvement according to their capital-saving or capital-using bias. Compare the best new design available for a consumption-sector plant with that of the last vintage in use (the two plants requiring the same amount of labour to operate them). The real cost of each plant consists of the services of investment-sector workers and plant, which we assume to be required in fixed proportions and to be of unchanging physical specification. With a given money-wage rate and rate of profit, this real cost is reflected in the money cost of production of each plant, along with the build-up of consumption-sector working capital necessary to get it into operation. When the money cost of a new plant (with its working capital) is the same as of the older one, and its potential service life the same, while its output is greater, the improvement is *neutral*.

The significance of this criterion can be expressed in two ways. If we measure the output of the investment sector in terms of units of productive capacity for use in the consumption-good sector (and units of productive capacity to produce units of productive capacity in the investment sector) then we can say that the improvement increases output per head equally in both sectors (that is, in the ratio that output per head of the consumption good is raised). Or we may measure the investment per man in terms of its real cost and say that the new technique has not changed the real-capital/labour ratio. (This criterion of neutrality is independent of what is actually going to happen to the rate of profit, and therefore to the relative shares of wages and profits in the value of output, as a result of the improvement.)

When the latest design reduces cost per unit of plant in terms of money (which reflects real physical cost) the improvement has a capital-saving bias. Output per head in the investment sector in terms of consumption-sector productive capacity has risen in a greater proportion than output her head in the consumption-good sector. Similarly, a higher cost per unit of plant implies a capital-using bias in the improvement.

An improvement in design which raises output both per head and per unit of real cost of plant creates a technique *superior* to any known before. A neutral improvement always means that the new design is superior to all those known hitherto, but this is not necessarily true of biased improvements. When the bias is so strong (in the capital-saving direction) as to reduce output per head in the consumption-good sector, or (in the capital-using direction) as to reduce output per unit of real cost of capital, the newest technique is not superior, in this sense, to the last one. Improvements of this kind may be called *partial* improvements; they lower one element in cost only by raising another.

If nothing better offers, it is worth while to make use of a partial improvement, introducing a design of plant with lower output per head, provided that (at the ruling rate of profit) the cost per plant is more than proportionately lower; or of a design which increases output per head in a smaller proportion than it raises cost per unit of plant, provided that the reduction in wages cost per unit of output is not less than the increase in capital cost per unit of output at the ruling rate of profit.

A new technique which satisfies this criterion is *eligible* at the ruling rate of profit, though not *superior* to all known techniques. A technique which (at the ruling rate of profit) reduces labour cost per unit of output by means of a proportionate addition to capital cost (or vice versa), compared to the best known hitherto, is *indifferent* to it at this rate of profit.

The Degree of Mechanisation

It is important to distinguish between bias in the course of technical progress and differences in the capital/labour ratio which may exist at a given phase of technical development.[1] At any one moment there may be a number of techniques available, none of which is superior to the rest. They can be represented on a productivity function drawn up on the basis of the prices ruling at that moment. Comparing possible techniques on the basis of the perpetual stream of net value of output that each promises, for a given investment of finance today, it is seen that a higher flow of future employment of labour per unit of investment is associated with a higher flow of output, and smaller employment with smaller output.

At the level of real wages actually ruling there may be only one technique that is eligible ; or there may be two, that with the higher employment promising a larger output just sufficient to pay the larger wages bill, while yielding the same profit on the investment. It would be possible for both techniques to be chosen for simultaneous schemes of investment, so that they will be operating side by side. There is then no difficulty in comparing the costs of the plants required for each, since the comparison is made at a common set of prices with a common cost of basic plant, and at a common rate of growth of the economy as a whole. The technique requiring more employment per unit of investment has a lower real-capital/labour ratio than the other. It is said to be of a lower *degree of mechanisation*. It is to be observed that we are here concerned with an *ex ante* productivity function consisting of sets of blueprints for possible techniques, from which a choice is made for new investment (including reinvestment of amortisation funds) at a moment of time.[2] Choices fall on the one, or on each of

---

[1] Recent controversies over the 'production function' have been much tangled by failure to make this distinction.

[2] It is not the same thing as an *ex post* production function in terms of output and the 'capital'/labour ratio in the economy as a whole. The latter does not represent choices to be made at a moment of time ; it is appropriate to a comparison between economies, each with its own past, that have developed at different rates of profit while having access to the same body of

the pair, that are eligible in the situation ruling when choices are made.

When the rate of profit has been constant in the past and is expected to remain so, we can identify the eligible techniques as those which are chosen at the ruling rate of profit. When the range of coexisting techniques is very finely graded, so that there is a small difference between the capital/labour ratios and the output/labour ratios of each pair of techniques eligible at a common rate of profit,[1] we can treat the pair as a single technique. On this basis we can say that there is a different degree of mechanisation corresponding to each level of the rate of profit.[2]

Notation

It is convenient to have a system of notation for comparing techniques. The letters Alpha, Beta etc. refer, in descending order, to the real-capital/labour ratio required for a technique (the overall rate of growth being given). Plus and minus refer to superiority and inferiority. Query-plus and query-minus refer to eligibility or ineligibility at a given rate of profit.[3]

Thus, taking a given steady rate of growth, and a given rate of profit which is expected to be constant in the future, we take our stand at Beta technique and compare other possibilities with it. Beta-plus is a superior technique, and Beta-minus an inferior technique, with the same real-capital/labour ratio as is required for Beta. Alpha-plus is a superior technique with a higher real-capital/labour ratio. Alpha-query-plus is a technique with a higher real-capital/labour ratio which would yield a higher rate of profit (at prices ruling in the Beta situation)

technical knowledge. Great confusion arises from confusing the *ex ante* production function with the succession of techniques chosen in the course of development through time. Cf. below, p. 132.

[1] The comparison must be made on the basis of a single rate of growth, since the rate of growth affects the age composition of the stock of basic plant, which affects the real cost of non-basic plant.

[2] The weary reader may complain that all this amounts to no more than the familiar doctrine that a higher ratio of capital to labour is associated with a lower rate of interest. But it is necessary to spell it out with care to understand what the familiar doctrine does and what it does not assert.

[3] These conventions are not quite the same as those used in my *Accumulation of Capital* because there I was comparing positions of equilibrium at different rates of profit.

but is not absolutely superior (at some higher rate of profit than that now ruling it would not be eligible). Gamma-query-minus is a technique with a lower real-capital/labour ratio that would yield a lower rate of profit, but is not absolutely inferior. And so forth.

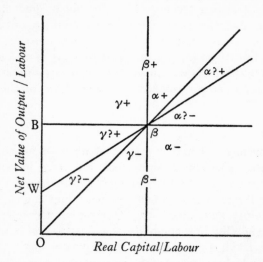

OB is net value of output per man at ruling prices with Beta technique
OW is the wage rate. WB is net profit per man employed.

A GOLDEN AGE

We now examine an economy in which smooth steady growth is going on. There is an autonomous steady rate of technical progress in the sense that new designs are introduced at equal intervals of time ; each new design raises output per head of consumption goods in a given proportion, compared to the last ; the real cost per plant (that is, per man employed in the consumption-good sector) remains constant as time goes by. In short, neutral technical progress is going on at a steady rate. The series of techniques being offered, as time goes by, are Beta-minus, Beta, Beta-plus, Beta-plus-plus etc.

Each firm is thinking in terms of perpetual expansion, but each is content to grow at the rate set by the overall growth rate of the economy.[1] Since we are assuming a constant labour force and a constant amount of employment, the overall growth rate is governed by the rate of technical progress. The firms are continually adjusting the money prices of consumption goods in such a way as to be able to sell the capacity output of the plant that they operate.

There is no saving out of wage incomes. The firms distribute to rentiers (as interest and dividends) a constant proportion of net profits, and, of what they receive, a constant proportion is spent on consumption goods.

Obsolescence

The length of working life of plant in the investment sector is determined by physical conditions ; we are assuming that one plant (with its team of workers) can turn out, successively, different kinds of consumption-sector plant ; it is versatile and therefore not subject to obsolescence.

A consumption-sector plant does suffer from obsolescence ; it is tied to one method of production and it has to face competition from younger, more productive rivals as it ages. If its physical life is long, it will be cut short by loss of profitability. Consider a situation in which (the money wage being constant) the price of the consumption good is falling steadily. When a particular consumption-sector plant is first produced, the output per man of its workers is higher than that of any who are operating older plants. A very small cut in price below that formerly ruling suffices to attract to it sufficient demand to set it running at capacity. The gross profit that it is earning is higher than that of older plants. A little later, newer plants have come into operation and a further cut in price has taken place. As it ages, the process goes on. Step by step, gross profit falls until the surplus of total receipts over the wage bill is only just sufficient to provide for profit at the current rate on working capital. The next fall in prices pushes the plant below the margin of profitability ; it retires from use, and (since consumption-good sector employment is being maintained) the team of men that it has been employing will be re-equipped

---

[1] In Harrod's language the 'warranted' rate of growth and the actual rate are both equal to the 'natural' rate of growth.

with a plant of the latest, most eligible, type. (It is the rise in the wage in terms of product that eats up gross profit. The above story was told in terms of prices falling ; it could equally well have been told in terms of money-wage rates rising relatively to the price of the consumption good.)

When the future earnings of a new plant are correctly estimated by the firm in charge of it, an obsolescence allowance is attached to it sufficient to recover, over its life, the original financial value of the investment. It is convenient to assume that all the types of consumption-sector plant that have been or will be invented have a longer potential physical life than they will actually realise, so that obsolescence is the only occasion of replacement.

Effective Demand

In these conditions, the real-wage rate rises at the same rate as output per head. The cost of labour in ·terms of his own product remains constant to each employer and the rate of profit on capital is constant. Consumption of workers and of rentier families rises in step with the rise of output of consumption goods. The whole economy remains in balance in the conditions of a golden age. The steady rise in demand keeps step with the steady rise in potential output and so keeps the economy at stretch. The expectations of profit on investment are continually fulfilled and therefore renewed. Investment is being maintained at a rate which permits the benefits of the technical progress to be realised.

The share of wages in total net income, and the ratio of the value of capital to net income are constant through time.

Valuations

There are some terminological puzzles that arise from the operation of the model in a golden age, even though it is perfectly clear what is assumed to be happening, both in real and in money terms.[1]

When technical progress is going on (with equilibrium continuously maintained) a constant rate of profit means either

[1] Cf. C. Kennedy, 'Technical Progress and Investment', *Economic Journal*, June 1961.

that the money-wage rate is rising or that the price of the consumption good is falling. We have chosen for convenience to assume a constant money-wage rate. The price of the consumption good is therefore falling as time goes by. The purchasing power of money cannot be constant both in terms of labour time and in terms of product, we therefore have to use a double standard of value.

Consider the effect of neutral technical progress, with a constant rate of profit, total employment being kept constant. Reckoning in terms of money, all incomes are constant. Annual gross profits in terms of money are constant. Every year some plants are retired and replaced by new ones of the same original value (a Beta-plus plant has the same cost as the Beta-minus . . . minus plant that it replaces). The money value of gross investment is constant. The money value of the stock of capital is constant. Looking at money values, we might be inclined to say that there is no net investment going on.

Whatever happens to money values, a physical index of capital will not show any particular change, since the number of plants is not altering and there is no reason to suppose that the later ones weigh any heavier than the earlier ones. All the same, total output is steadily expanding.

When we reckon in terms of the consumption good, we see that all incomes are rising at the same rate as output per head. Plants of a given money cost (reflecting real cost in terms of labour-time at the ruling rate of profit) have a rising value in terms of product as the real-wage rate rises. (A Beta-plus plant has a value higher than that of a Beta one in proportion to the rate of growth.) The wealth of rentiers rises in proportion to income. The annual value of gross investment rises in the same proportion, and the net value of investment is equal to the annual increment in the value of capital. Either way, the share of profit in the value of output is constant. Annual profit on capital is the rise in the value in terms of consumption goods of the stock of capital that takes place over a year, plus the consumption of rentiers. The rate of profit on capital is the ratio of this quantity to the value of capital in terms of consumption goods.

The device of keeping the money-wage rate constant and

permitting prices to fall is, of course, merely a device. We are not concerned with the real-life reactions of individuals in such a situation.[1] We are using the constant purchasing power of money (at a given rate of profit) over labour-time as an X-ray to permit us to see what is happening in terms of real costs as technical progress goes on.

In golden-age conditions the rentiers are spending the whole of their money receipts. The rise in the value of their wealth, and of their annual saving, in terms of consumption goods, is proportional to the rise in the purchasing power of money over consumption goods; that is, to the golden-age growth rate of the economy. Saving in terms of money is no longer required ; the golden age must be conceived to have emerged from an earlier state of affairs when real-capital accumulation was going on. The firms are paying interest and dividends to rentiers on the finance made available to them during that phase. The rentiers are now sharing in the growth of the economy which is taking place as the result of technical progress.[2] Our X-ray device of keeping money-wage rates constant makes the situation visualised in the model perfectly perspicuous, but there is a possibility of verbal dispute as to whether the conduct of rentiers should be described as 'saving', 'abstinence', or merely as refraining from consuming capital gains.

We can use our X-ray all the more conveniently if we eliminate complications due to time lags. Let us suppose that the various firms stagger their pay days for wages over the week, and for interest and dividends over the year, so that a regular stream of daily payments is made in terms of money. The sales of consumption goods are also assumed to be spread evenly over the year. Thus payments and receipts, for the firms taken as a whole, are equal to each other at a constant daily rate in the conditions of the golden age.

The Meaning of the Golden Age

To set out the characteristics of a golden age by no means implies a prediction that it is likely to be realised in any actual

---

[1] Cf. p. 70, above.
[2] The *Model for the Future* (p. 17, *et seq.*) sets out this situation in an extreme form.

period of history. The concept is useful, rather, as a means of distinguishing various types of disharmony that are liable to arise in an uncontrolled economy.

Three types of conditions in which a golden age cannot be realised are discussed in what follows : bias in technical progress, changeability in the tempo of technical progress, and disharmony between the rate of accumulation of capital and the rate of growth of output which technical progress makes possible.

BIASED PROGRESS

The effects of biased progress are somewhat complicated ; we tackle the problem in two stages. We examine it first subject to the arbitrary assumption that investment is carried on in such a way as to preserve full employment without excess demand for labour. Later we will consider how the demand for labour is affected by it.

Temporary and Persistent Bias

Consider the situation when, one year, the most eligible technique offered requires a higher real cost (in labour-time) per plant (that is, per team of men in the consumption-good sector) than that which is due to be replaced. To carry out this investment in such a way as to make it possible to maintain full employment in the future requires some extra workers with the appropriate basic plant to be directed to producing consumption-sector plant. One round of such investment could be made by diverting labour and basic plant from replacing basic plant. If so, there will be a deficiency of basic plant in the future. When bias in technical progress is merely a passing wobble that will be compensated later on by a wobble the other way (a round of inventions which offer an eligible technique with a lower real cost per plant), then an opportunity will occur to make good the deficit in basic plant without disturbing the balance of employment between the sectors.

When, over a run of years, the pace of technical progress remains constant and there is a compensation of the biases one way and the other, the general effect might be described as imperfectly neutral or near-enough neutrality. When the other conditions are satisfied, we could then have a near-enough golden age.

When there has been perfect neutrality up to a certain date, and then bias is introduced which remains at the same level thereafter (the pace of progress remaining the same), the maintenance of full employment would involve a gradual change-over to a higher real-capital/labour ratio, which, when it has been completed, settles down to neutrality once more.

Let us suppose that such a transition is carried out. In terms of our notation (taking for simplicity a length of service life of plant of three periods only), Beta-minus-minus and Beata-minus plant have the same real cost per plant. Alpha has a higher real cost. Alpha-plus has the same real cost per plant as Alpha, and so will have those drawn from all later techniques. Thus when Alpha, Alpha-plus and Alpha-plus-plus plants have been installed, the transition has been made to a new golden age with a higher real-capital/labour ratio than the former one (*ex hypothesi* the growth rates are the same in each).

In the new golden age, the ratio of the labour force in the investment sector to that in the consumption-good sector is higher than in the old one, and the stock of basic plant is larger. During the transition, therefore, there must have been a period when gross investment was directed to building new basic plants. While this was going on, the output of consumption goods was growing at less than the golden age rate (it may have actually fallen for a time).

We are basing our discussion on purely autonomous technical change. The bias is something that occurs for technical reasons and there is nothing to be done about it. We can, however, compare the new golden age with the old one, and say whether the switch-over represented a true or only a partial improvement. If it was a true improvement the output/real-capital ratio rose during the process of transition.

Notation

Type of plant	$\beta -$	a	γ
Output per plant	$b -$	a	c
Real cost per plant	k_b	k_a	k_c

A true improvement with capital-using bias is seen when
$$\frac{a}{b-} > \frac{k_a}{k_b}.$$

Capital-saving bias entails a fall in real cost per plant (k_c is less than k_b). A transition from one golden age to another which is relatively capital-saving involves a movement of labour out of the investment sector into the consumption-good sector. The movement represents a true improvement provided that output per plant is not reduced during the switch over ; that is, provided that c is not less than $b-$. A sufficient increase in output per man is required to offset a capital-using bias, whereas any increase at all in output per man makes a capital-saving technique superior.

Now, suppose that each new technique is capital-using compared to the last in a regular way, so that the succession offered runs from Gamma-minus to Beta to Alpha-plus. If the economy were adjusted to maintaining full employment in these conditions, the stock of basic plant would be adjusted to making a continuous increase in itself and labour would be continuously drawn out of the consumption-good sector into the investment sector. To represent true improvements, the series of techniques would have to offer a *proportionately* greater step-up in output per plant at each round. This, of course, is not logically impossible, but it appears to be a very implausible state of affairs. It seems more reasonable to expect continuous capital-using bias in a situation in which progress is gradually petering out so that, after a time, true improvements will no longer be offered. On the other hand, continuous capital-saving bias would be rather too good to be true.

After a period of heavy bias in the capital-using direction, opportunities are thrown up for capital-saving inventions. Thus near-enough neutrality over the long run seems to be what we might in general expect to see.

Constant Marginal Productivity

There is a special case of highly capital-using bias which, though not at all plausible, has a certain scholastic interest. This is the case in which each successive technique offered is indifferent to the last. Beta succeeds Gamma, and Alpha succeeds Beta. The additional output per plant (that is, per man employed in the consumption-good sector) is just sufficient to provide for profit at the ruling rate on the additional capital. When r is the rate of profit,

$$(b - c) = r(k_b - k_c)$$
$$(a - b) = r(k_a - k_b)$$

and so forth.

The marginal efficiency of investment for the individual firm is the same thing as the rate of profit on additional capital. For the economy as a whole, it is the ratio of the additional output of a given labour force to the value of the additional investment that makes it possible. In this special case the two are equal.

The Wicksell Process

The normal treatment of accumulation in neo-classical doctrine, as worked out in particular by Wicksell, is subject to the assumption of 'given technical knowledge'. All the possibilities are already laid out in a book of blue-prints and no new inventions or discoveries are made. At any given rate of profit, the most eligible technique has already been installed throughout the economy, and full employment obtains. The only way in which accumulation can continue is then by moving to techniques which are eligible only at a lower rate of profit (in the direction Beta to Alpha-query-minus). The neo-classical story is that accumulation takes the form of gradually raising the real-capital/labour ratio, passing through a continuous series of techniques with a gradually falling rate of profit on capital. It is not easy to see how this could come about in an unregulated private-enterprise economy.[1]

For a planned economy with a constant labour force the limit of eligibility of technique is not reached until the marginal product of investment is zero. But a planned economy with all technical possibilities already known, would be well advised to take a short-cut (at least for the longer-lived investments) to the most eligible technique, rather than to pass through a continuous series of less eligible ones.

[1] See below, p. 132.

A Model of Technical Progress

Neither way does the neo-classical analysis make sense when it is applied to a process going on through time. It seems to have arisen from a confusion between a process of accumulation and a comparison between positions each in static equilibrium at a different rate of profit.[1]

Bias and Investment

So far we have considered how the situation would develop if various types of technical change were implemented in such a way as to preserve full employment. This was a perfectly arbitrary assumption. What actually happens must depend upon how firms react to the form that progress takes. When technical progress is neutral, it is only necessary for each firm to keep the value of its capital constant (in terms of labour-time) and all collectively are maintaining full employment at a constant rate of profit, with the real-wage rate rising in proportion to output per head. With biased progress these conditions cannot all be satisfied.

When firms about to replace, say, Beta-minus-minus plant find that Alpha is now the most eligible technique and devote to it the same sum (with constant money-wage rates) as the old plant originally cost, they will acquire fewer plants, offering less employment, for Alpha technique requires a higher real cost per man employed in the consumption-good sector. Consequently employment in the consumption-good sector will fall, and the resulting reduction in consumption by workers will reduce receipts of the firms as a whole and precipitate slumpy conditions.

If the firms decide to replace the Beta-minus-minus plant with an equal number of Alpha plants, offering the same employment, an excess demand for labour will develop ; demands upon the investment sector have increased while employment offered in the consumption-good sector has not been reduced.

It is possible to imagine an intermediate policy which keeps employment constant, so that labour is released from the

<hr />

[1] Or perhaps, confusion with the *ex ante* production function facing an individual firm at the moment when technique is chosen. Cf. above, p. 92, note 2.

consumption-good sector at just the rate required to provide for the increase in gross investment necessary to implement the capital-using bias in technique.

Conversely, with capital-saving bias, a policy of keeping the real value of capital constant would precipitate a boom and a policy of keeping consumption-sector employment constant would precipitate a slump. The intermediate policy that just preserves a constant demand for labour involves a release of labour from the investment sector accompanied by a corresponding increase in employment in the consumption-good sector.

Bias and Thriftiness

Let us suppose, for the sake of argument, that biased progress is implemented in conditions of full employment. Then the ratio of gross investment to consumption is raised by capital-using bias and reduced by capital-saving bias. We have to consider the effect of this upon saving. To do so, we continue to make use of our X-ray device of keeping money-wage rates constant.

When full employment is maintained, the money-wage bill remains constant whether workers are moving from sector to sector or not. Now, suppose that the firms continue to pay out the same sums of money to rentiers whatever happens, and that the rentiers continue to spend what they receive on consumption goods. During a transition period when workers are moving into the investment sector, the output of consumer goods is rising less fast than the output per head (and, as we saw, may even fall for a time). The rentiers and the workers maintain the same relative share in consumption whatever happens, prices falling, and consumption per unit of money expenditure rising, slower or faster, in step with the output of consumption goods.

What is happening, in effect, in this situation, is that the firms taken collectively are financing the investment that they feel called upon to make by retaining profits. In the case of capital-using bias they are imposing thriftiness upon the rentiers to just the extent required to look after the additional investment that is being undertaken. When the bias is in the capital-saving direction, they are allowing the rentiers to consume the capital that is being saved.

When a transition has been made in this way from one golden age to another with the same growth rate and a higher real-capital/labour ratio, the rate of profit on capital has been lowered. Since the wage rate has been raised in the same proportion as the output of consumer goods, gross profit per man, averaged over the labour force as a whole, has risen in the same proportion, but the value of capital per man has risen in a greater proportion.[1] Conversely, the rate of profit, in these conditions, is raised by capital-saving bias. In so far as there is a choice of degrees of mechanisation at each round of technical progress, this tends to reinforce the bias.

At the other extreme, if firms pay out to rentiers, and rentiers consume, the same proportion of gross profits as before, the rate of profit is raised by capital-using and lowered by capital-saving bias. (The effect of selecting the appropriate degree of mechanisation at each round then mitigates, instead of reinforcing, the bias.)

It is possible to imagine an intermediate policy which keeps the rate of profit constant, though there does not seem to be any particular reason to expect the firms to hit upon it.

If the rate of profit were the same after a transition has been completed, the share of wages in the value of output is less where the bias is capital-using and greater where it is capital-saving. Valuing capital and net income in terms of consumption goods, the overall capital/income ratio has been raised by a capital-using transition and lowered by a capital-saving one.

When the appropriate policy is pursued, under both heads, so that full employment is preserved with a constant rate of profit, continuous bias is associated with a continuous fall or rise in the share of wages in the value of output, and a continuous rise or fall in the overall capital/income ratio.

A steady rate of growth of output of consumption goods accompanied by a continuous steady change in the capital/income ratio, at a constant rate of profit, may be described as a

---

[1] This is subject to the proviso that the real capital per man in the investment sector is not very much less than in the consumption-good sector.

quasi-golden age.[1] This concept, however, depends upon very far-fetched assumptions, as the foregoing argument has shown. It has none of the solid simplicity of a golden age proper.

UNSTEADY PROGRESS

When there is a jump in technical progress in the sense that the latest designs for consumption-sector plant are a greater improvement than has been the case before (in the notation used above $\frac{(b+) - (b)}{(b)}$ appreciably exceeds $\frac{(b) - (b-)}{(b-)}$) provided that competition between firms is strong enough to keep prices falling with costs, there is a more rapid fall in prices (a faster rise in real wages) than before, and some of the older plant becomes obsolete faster than was expected on the basis of past experience.

A similar situation would arise if some firms, growing more aggressive than formerly in competition, try to steal a march on the others by replacing plant earlier than formerly.

Firms caught out by an unexpected fall in prices make losses, in the sense that they have to write off plant that has not fully returned its initial cost. But if they refuse to be pushed out of business, and if they can find the necessary finance, they now respond to the challenge by replacing the obsolete plant. The result is an increased demand for new plant. An investment boom develops.

Conversely, slumpy conditions set in when technical progress slows down or competition grows more slack.

We must consider the reaction of changes in the pace of investment upon the choice of technique from those available at any moment.

When there is enough labour available to allow a boom to run its course, a higher rate of profit makes less mechanised techniques eligible.

If near-full employment prevailed before the boom developed, an inflationary situation is precipitated, there is a scarcity

---

[1] Cf. my *Accumulation of Capital*, chap. 17. The argument is there conducted on the assumption of no rentier consumption, which simplifies it a great deal.

of labour, and our convenient assumption of constant money-wage rates becomes untenable. In the turbulence of an out-of-equilibrium situation there is no simple generalisation to be made, but it would certainly be unreasonable to expect less mechanised techniques to be selected by firms engaged in a scramble for labour.[1] Conversely, in slumpy conditions, if firms react to the level of real wages rather than to the state of the labour supply, more mechanised techniques tend to be chosen, which reduces employment offered by a given real value of capital.[2]

All such arguments, however, are somewhat fanciful, for when the economy has run off the rails of steady growth, no simple story can be told about how it will behave. Nor would it be possible in practical investigations to draw a distinction between changes in the real-capital/labour ratio due to bias in technical progress from those due to changes in the degree of mechanisation ; or between changes in the pace of investment due to changes in the pace of progress and those due to any other cause of changes in expectations.

The fact that technical progress is liable to be unsteady and is therefore unpredictable has a tendency to increase thriftiness. Prudent firms prefer to err on the safe side and like to write off plant in a financial sense before it actually becomes obsolete. This tends to make amortisation allowances higher and what is counted as distributable net profit so much the lower ; it thus has a tendency to reduce the rate of profit associated with any given rate of growth.

The greater riskiness of more unsteady technical progress might be held to discourage accumulation, but on the other hand it might also be held to give a spur to competition.

SURPLUS AND SCARCITY OF LABOUR

In the golden age the stock of capital is already such as to offer employment to the available labour force, and accumulation is keeping up with technical progress (which is neutral

---

[1] *Ibid.* 'The Concertina Effect', p. 203.

[2] On this basis, a slump precipitated by unemployment resulting from capital-using bias without an appropriate increase in gross investment (see above p. 103) would lead to a higher degree of mechanisation, reinforcing the capital-using tendency and making unemployment all the greater.

and steady) in such a way as to maintain full employment.

We must now consider situations in which this happy harmony between demand and supply of labour fails to obtain.

Lack of Energy

Organised industry may be offering more or less constant employment in conditions of a near-enough golden age (with steady technical progress going on) so far as its own sector of the economy is concerned, while surrounded by a low-level self-subsistence sector whose workers would be only too glad to take service with the industrial firms if they could.

In such a situation, the failure of employment to increase is sometimes blamed, in popular argument, on the technical progress taking place in organised industry. Investment is going into raising output per head in that sector (say, substituting Beta-plus for Beta-minus plant). Would it not be better to stop the progress and put investment into employing more labour at a constant level of output per head (retaining Beta technique and increasing the number of Beta plants) ?

Such an argument, of course, is fallacious. The trouble does not lie in technical progress but in an insufficiency of investment. If the firms could be induced to carry out sufficient investment and training of labour to expand the organised sector at such a rate as to keep the level of wages constant within it, from some base date, then every increase in productivity would be accompanied by a rise in the ratio of investment to consumption. The faster was technical progress, the more rapid would be the acceleration of accumulation. (All the more so if rentier consumption were prevented from increasing.)

When such a policy is pursued by the firms, obsolescence is brought to an end. The length of service life of plant is increased up to the physical limit. Older types are kept running, working side by side with later types, the labour force being expanded correspondingly. At the same time the rate of profit is rising so that less mechanised techniques are becoming eligible. (Successive techniques go in the direction Alpha, Beta-plus, Gamma-plus-plus.[1]) Both movements help to

[1] This is a near-enough type of argument, for our system of notation can be accurately used only when the rate of profit and the rate of growth of the economy are constant.

speed up the absorption of workers into organised industry, for now gross investment is going into setting up additional plants, instead of replacing obsolete plants by superior ones, and each round of investment creates plants offering more employment per unit of real cost.

This is upon the assumption that the firms are guided in their choice of technique by the current rate of profit. Since the rate of profit is changing and is higher than it will be after full employment has been reached, mistaken investments will be made on this basis. It would be better, in principle, to carry out the whole programme on a rational plan. But it would never be better to install an inferior technique when a superior one is available.

Lack of Finance

Insufficient investment may be due not so much to lack of energy in existing firms (or would-be new entrants to industry) as to difficulties in securing finance. When firms differ amongst themselves in energy and in success, discrepancies arise between the distribution of plans for investment and command over finance. For instance, the most energetic firms may be the youngest, while the greatest financial resources are accruing to the oldest. A progressive difficulty in obtaining finance prevents a golden age from being maintained even when all other conditions are right for it.[1]

The uncertainty and instability associated with technical progress might be held to make finance harder to come by ; but against this must be set its appeal to the gambling instinct.

There is a special problem of finance connected with capital-using bias in technical progress. To replace an obsolete plant by one of greater cost involves an expenditure of new finance, over and above the reinvestment of the finance originally committed. This is true even when money outlays of the firms as a whole remain constant, in the manner described above. By causing some labour to be transferred from the consumption-good to the investment sector, the firm (without, of course, any conscious intention) is raising profit margins all round. (A smaller quantity of consumption goods is now selling for the

---

[1] This is a form of the 'inherent vice' discussed above, p. 77.

same total daily outlay by consumers.) Since it does not itself get more than a small share of the benefit of this additional profit, it has to finance the investment partly by borrowing (directly or through the banking system) sums equivalent to the savings that its investment is generating.

To put the same point in another way, the Beta-minus plant to be replaced has not got to its credit a sufficient amortisation fund to pay for Alpha plant that will employ the same amount of labour. The firm must find some additional finance to carry out the change. If it cannot get the funds, or cannot get them except upon onerous terms, the employment that it offers will be reduced.[1] It certainly will install Alpha-type plant, for that is now the most eligible, but it will install less Alpha plant than corresponds to the Beta-minus plant withdrawn. The consequent reduction in its outlay on wages reduces receipts for other firms, and so precipitates a recession.

This is an extremely important and serious drawback connected with capital-using bias in technical progress ; conversely, an important advantage of capital-saving bias.

Lack of Competition

When technical progress (whether neutral or biased) is raising output per head and money incomes are constant, then, if prices also remain constant, the physical quantity of goods sold remains constant. In this situation the only effect of technical progress is to reduce employment.

In a less extreme form this is a potent cause of what, in popular argument, is regarded as technological unemployment. The trouble arises, however, not from the technical progress but from the stickiness of prices.[2]

Scarcity of Labour

When firms are energetic, finance adequate and competition keen, the pressure to accumulate may be so strong as to run up against the barrier set by full employment.

For purposes of our simple model we have taken technical progress to be completely autonomous, in the sense that the

---

[1] The position is analogous to the case of rising money-wage rates discussed above, p. 72, though not identical with it.

[2] Cf. above, p. 18.

firms have no control over it. This assumption cannot be maintained in such conditions.

When firms see profitable markets all around but cannot get hands to increase production, they have a strong motive to increase the rate at which innovations are introduced and to encourage fresh inventions to be made. A scarcity of labour thus has a tendency to increase the rate of technical progress. In such a situation the firms would not reject capital-using inventions and might even merely increase the degree of mechanisation (moving in the direction Beta to Alpha-query-minus) if no other way of increasing productivity offered. But there is no reason why the improvements sought out in these conditions should not be near-enough neutral.[1]

CONCLUSION

The austere assumptions of our simple model and our X-ray device of keeping money-wage rates constant make the foregoing analysis unlifelike. Nevertheless the relationships that they enable us to uncover seem to correspond to those that can be vaguely perceived through the fog of index-number ambiguities that hangs over real problems.

It must be remembered, however, that in our analysis technical progress was assumed to have no effect upon either the nature of commodities or the character of workers and consumers. When it is discussed in a wider setting other considerations have to be brought into the account.

APPENDIX

(1) *The Criterion of Neutrality*

Various criteria have been proposed for the neutrality of technical progress, as between labour and capital, in connection

[1] Cf. above, p. 15.

with various theories of distribution and accumulation. To reduce them to common terms, they may be set out in the form of a comparison between stationary economies, with zero accumulation, each of which has settled down to using the profit-maximising technique selected from its own book of blue-prints. The relation between the thriftiness conditions in the economies is such that they can be in stationary equilibrium with the same rate of profit, in spite of having different incomes.

Our criterion of neutrality is that (over the relevant range of rates of profits) the respective techniques eligible in two economies at the same rate of profit require the same real-capital/labour ratio (real capital being the total stock of capital measured by its cost reckoned in terms of labour-time).

When this condition is satisfied, and the rates of profit actually are equal, the real-wage rate in the economy with the superior technique is higher in the same ratio as net output (which we take to consist of a homogeneous consumption good), and the relative shares of wages and profits in output are the same in the two economies. If the condition of neutrality is satisfied but rates of profit are not the same in the two economies, relative shares may go either way, since, within each economy considered separately, a lower rate of profit (and consequently higher degree of mechanisation of technique) may be associated with either a higher or a lower net profit per man employed.

Pigou[1] divides 'improvements' into those which are 'labour saving' and those which are 'capital saving'. This leaves undistinguished all those that involve a higher rate of output both per unit of labour and per unit of 'capital'. It may be taken to mean, in our terminology, a distinction between partial improvements at each end, leaving all fully superior techniques in one bag.

Professor Hicks[2] describes a neutral 'improvement' as one which raises the marginal productivity of labour and of 'capital', each in the same proportion, when the ratio of labour to 'capital' is constant. He seems not to have been aware of the ambiguity involved in comparing stocks of capital existing in situations with different wage rates ; we have to find out what

---

[1] *Economics of Welfare*, Part IV, chap. IV.
[2] *Wages*, p. 121.

meaning of the ratio of 'capital' to labour best fits the sense of his argument.

Hicks identifies the marginal product of capital with the rate of profit. Then, taking product in its natural sense, as a quantity of output, capital must be measured in units of output. Or, if capital is measured in terms of labour-time, the marginal product must be divided by the real-wage rate, so as to reduce it also to terms of labour-time.

Now, when the ratio to labour of capital measured in labour-time is the same in two economies, and their rates of profit are equal, while the real-wage rate is higher in the superior economy in the same proportion as output, then the marginal net product of labour (which Hicks identifies with the real wage) and the marginal product in terms of output of capital in terms of labour-time are higher, in the superior economy, in equal proportions, for both are higher in the same proportion as the real-wage rate. Thus Hicks's criterion of neutrality is satisfied. His criterion, therefore, comes to the same thing as ours.

Harrod[1] specifies neutrality as that which keeps the capital/income ratio constant when the rate of profit is constant, capital being measured by its value in terms of the consumption good. This also agrees with ours. (Indeed, our definition was evolved, in the first instance, to satisfy this requirement.)

Others have proposed criteria that run in terms of the marginal productivity not of 'capital' but of physical capital goods. Amongst these the easiest to understand is Professor Meade's,[2] for he does not complicate his picture by any attempt to make it look plausible.

The factors of production are labour and machines of a single type which somehow has the same identity when its productivity varies. The ranges of possible techniques in the two economies (the two books of blue-prints) each consist in a continuous variation in the machine/labour ratio, both for producing machines and for producing the homogeneous consumption good, the marginal product per unit of labour rising, in each sector, and the marginal product per machine falling, as the machine/labour ratio rises. There is no form

---

[1] *Towards a Dynamic Economics*, p. 23.
[2] *A Neo-classical Theory of Economic Growth*.

of capital except machines. In each economy, the machine/labour ratios in the two sectors are chosen so that marginal productivity per machine in the machine sector is equal to the rate of profit and the marginal product of labour in the consumption-good sector is equal to the real wage.

Since we are comparing stationary states, the annual output of machines in each economy is equal to annual replacements required to keep the stock intact. It is assumed that replacements required are proportional to the number of machines in existence; the two stocks of machines measured by cost reckoned in terms of labour-time are therefore proportional to the cost of the respective rates of output of machines, also reckoned in terms of labour-time; the value of each stock of machines in terms of the consumption good is its cost multiplied by the real-wage rate ruling in the economy to which it belongs.

Now, Meade's criterion of neutrality is that 'with unchanged supplies of all factors, the marginal product of every factor is raised in the same proportion'.[1] If 'supplies of factors' were taken to mean the overall machine/labour ratio, and the rise in productivity was confined to the production of the consumption good, then this criterion would come to the same as ours, for, with no difference in the cost of producing machines, our real-capital/labour ratio corresponds to Meade's machine/labour ratio.

It seems, however, that Meade intends 'supplies of factors' to apply to the machine/labour ratio in each sector separately, and the rise in productivity to apply to the production of machines as well as to the production of the consumption good.

When the cost of a machine (reckoned in terms of labour-time) is lower in the superior economy, then if the overall machine/labour ratio is the same (when the rate of profit is the same), there is a strong capital-saving bias in the relation between the two techniques and the share of profit in income is lower in the superior economy. Our condition of neutrality would require that, when the rate of profit is the same in the two economies, the number of machines per man (averaged over both sectors taken together) should be greater in the superior economy in the same ratio as the cost per machine is less.

[1] *Op. cit.* p. 39.

This condition would be satisfied if, first, the production functions have an elasticity of substitution equal to unity, so that a lower labour cost per machine causes a proportionate increase in the machine/labour ratio in each sector separately, and second, either the division of the labour force between the sectors is the same in the two economies or the machine/labour ratio happens to be identical in the two sectors in each economy.

Meade recognises that these assumptions (or some equivalent) are necessary to secure constant relative shares, but his condition for neutrality is only that the machine-labour production function for producing machines and that for producing the consumer good are both higher in the superior economy, each isoelastically with its opposite number in the inferior economy. This is compatible with what, from our point of view, is capital-saving or capital-using bias; and may be associated with a higher or lower share of wages in the superior economy, according as the overall machine/labour ratio is increased in a smaller or greater proportion than the labour cost per machine is reduced. His criterion is 'void for uncertainty'.

Meade claims that Hicks belongs to his party; but Hicks's criterion is intended to be sufficient to guarantee constant relative shares, whereas to satisfy the traditional requirement of neutrality, Meade's has to be buttressed by further provisos. Moreover, whatever Hicks may have meant by 'capital', there is no ground for suspecting him of having anticipated the invention of Meade's machine.

(2) *The Cobb-Douglas Production Function*

The text-book analysis of accumulation and technical progress is usually presented in terms of a production function in output, 'capital' and labour, moving in the output dimension at a steady rate through time. It is often depicted as a Cobb-Douglas function, which has the special property that the relative shares of labour and 'capital' in the value of output are the same, at each moment of time at all labour/'capital' ratios.

Let us grant for the sake of argument that there exists at

each moment a complete set of ready-drawn blue-prints for a variety of techniques. We must now suppose that the whole set is changing in a regular way, each batch being scrapped as soon as a superior batch has been drawn. The firms select from each batch the technique which (at the ruling rate of profit) offers the biggest saving in cost compared to the best of the last batch.

When technical progress is neutral, the curve in output, labour and value of capital at the ruling rate of profit, representing the latest set of blue-prints, is rising isoelastically — that is without change in its elasticity at points corresponding to equal capital/output ratios. Then, provided that accumulation goes on in such a way as to keep the rate of profit constant, the relative shares of wages and profits are constant. This has nothing whatever to do with the shape of the curve. It depends entirely on the relative positions of the points representing iso-profit techniques as the curve rises ; and this is the same whatever shape it may have.

When there is a capital-using bias in the successive series of sets of blue-prints and the rate of profit remains constant, the relative share of profit is rising. Conversely for the opposite bias. This has nothing to do with the shape of the curves. It arises from the fact that bias introduces a change into the composition of gross output, raising or lowering the proportion of capital goods to consumer goods. A production function drawn up simply in terms of 'output' does not make any sense unless the physical composition of output can be specified.

There is a quite different kind of question to which the Cobb-Douglas function can be applied, that is, a comparison between economies having a series of books of blue-prints in common, but developing along different paths, with different rates of profit.

To make sense of this we have to conceive of a number of economies, separate from each other, all passing through the same phases of technical progress. But a given phase of technical development — that is, a given book of blue-prints — is represented by a different productivity curve for each rate of growth (with different rates of growth the composition of the stock of capital is different) and for each rate of profit (with different rates of profit, relative prices of different products are liable to be different). One phase of technical progress must therefore be represented by families of curves corresponding to different growth rates and rates of profit. To postulate that a number of economies are passing through the same phases of technical progress means that the whole set of curves is rising in a regular way.

We cannot say anything definite about the relative capital/ labour ratios in the various economies, for each is attached to a different member of the set of curves, though there may be a general presumption that a series of more mechanised techniques is being chosen where the rate of profit is lower. The shape of each curve, taken by itself, tells us nothing about how the relative shares compare in economies each attached to a different curve. To find this out, we should have to know both the physical, technical characteristics represented by points on a single curve, and the value relations between the curves. The 'capital' in the traditional production function is neither fish, flesh nor good red herring. It mixes up the physical and the value relations and cannot tell us anything about either.

(3) *Kaldor's Technical Progress Function*

Kaldor's technical progress function[1] depicts a state of affairs in which (with a constant labour force) it is physically possible to carry out steady growth at *any* rate. At low rates of growth, there is a capital-saving bias in the succession of techniques and at high rates, a capital-using bias ; there is a regular succession of degrees of bias, first less capital-saving and then more capital-using, corresponding to higher and higher rates of accumulation. At one rate of growth neutral progress obtains.

Kaldor passes blithely over the troublesome problem of the behaviour of gross and net saving with biased progress and takes it for granted that a constant rate of accumulation of capital is associated with a constant rate of profit. Thus, his

[1] 'A Model of Economic Growth', *Economic Journal*, December 1957, and *Essays on Economic Stability and Growth*.

technical progress function indicates one golden age and a continuous series of quasi-golden ages, with different degrees of bias either way. This series is expressed merely in terms of growth rates and apparently applies equally at any level of the initial capital/labour ratio.

It has sometimes been argued that this conception contains a text-book type of production function concealed within itself, but this is certainly not the case. True, it can be deduced from the function that, if we compare economies, whatever their rates of growth, which have different capital/labour ratios, the one with the higher capital/labour ratio at a particular moment also has higher output per head at that moment ; but there is no common set of blue-prints from which the firms in each are choosing, and they have certainly not chosen their techniques according to the text-book doctrine, so that a higher capital/output ratio corresponds to a lower rate of profit. Indeed, in Kaldor's system this doctrine is meaningless, for at any except one critical value of the rate of growth, the capital/output ratio is continuously changing through time in any one economy, with a constant rate of profit. It is true that, if we compare different economies at a particular moment, the one with the higher capital/output ratio has the slower rate of growth and therefore the lower rate of profit, but this is due to another feature of the model and has no connection with any functional relationship between the rate of profit and the choice of technique.

What has to be accounted for is that slower growth is associated with a faster *rate of fall* in the capital/output ratio (or, above the critical value, faster growth with a faster *rate of rise*). Kaldor postulates that the output of the individual firm, at any moment, is limited by labour. In such a case, we have argued, the firms most keen to grow will be most keen to find superior techniques ; any bias there might be, for technical reasons, in the series of improvements they would try to offset by finding still better improvements. But if slower growth is due to greater difficulty in getting finance, there is a good reason why the firms in a slower growing economy should be more keen to find capital-saving improvements, which permit the output of the given labour force to be raised at a smaller cost in terms of gross investment. When finance is easy, there

Appendix

is no impediment to adopting the most superior techniques that offer, even if they have a capital-using bias.

It seems very strange, however (and not at all consonant with Kaldor's general point of view), that the strength of the urge to accumulate should have no effect on the pace (as opposed to the bias) of technical progress.

IV

A NEO-NEOCLASSICAL THEOREM

WHEN the conception of the rate of profit determined by the
rate of accumulation of capital and thriftiness conditions is
combined with the conception of a choice of technique from a
given spectrum of possibilities, it can be seen that the highest
rate of output of consumption goods is achieved when the rate
of profit on capital is equal to the rate of accumulation.[1]

INTRODUCTION

We make our usual simplifying assumptions. The type
of economy with which the argument is concerned is a closed
system, with no government sector and no self-employed
producers. All activity is organised in capitalist firms. There
are two classes of households, each homogeneous within itself —
workers who receive wages and rentiers who receive profits.
Total net income is exhaustively divided into wages and profits.
Consumption goods never change in respect to their specifica-
tions or the proportions in which they are consumed. (This is
equivalent to assuming a single homogeneous consumption
good.) There are no scarce factors of production or economies
of scale to industry. Competition prevails in the sense that
there is a uniform rate of profit on capital in all lines of production and at all stages of production. Perfect tranquillity prevails
and present conditions are confidently expected to last for the
indefinite future.

All values are reckoned in terms of money at a constant
money-wage rate.

Prices and Profits
The money-wage rate being given, normal prices for each kind

---

[1] For the history of this theorem see below, p. 135.

of output, at every stage of production, are determined by technical conditions and the rate of profit.[1]

The level of prices, and therefore of profits, is such that net saving per annum per unit of capital is equal to net investment per annum per unit of capital, that is, to the rate of accumulation. When all wage incomes are spent for consumption, the rate of profit on capital is then determined by the rate of accumulation and the proportion of profits saved. A higher rate of accumulation, with a given propensity to save, entails a higher rate of profit. A higher propensity to save, with a given rate of accumulation, entails a lower rate of profit.

P is profit per annum.
I is value of net investment per annum.
K is the value of the stock of capital goods at normal prices.
s_p is the proportion of profits saved.

$$P = \frac{1}{s_p} I. \quad \frac{P}{K} = \frac{\frac{1}{s_p} I}{K}.$$

I/K is the rate of accumulation. P/K is the rate of profit on capital.

With any given rate of physical output per man employed, prices are lower, and therefore the real-wage rate higher, the lower the rate of profit on capital.

THE DEGREE OF MECHANISATION

One aspect of our proposition concerns the selection of more or less 'capital-intensive' techniques from a given body of knowledge. The problem is artificial, for we have to compare equilibrium positions each with its own future and its own past. (A process of changing the capital structure of an economy is a very different matter.) We have to compare economies, each in a state of equilibrium, at different points on a given spectrum of techniques. There is no connection between them except that they have access to the same book of blue-prints describing the known techniques of production.

[1] Cf. p. 10.

E*

An economy is in equilibrium when the techniques in use are such that no individual firm could get a better rate of profit on its capital by using some other technique, given present and expected prices. To compare one technique with another for the economy as a whole, we have to consider the net output that each permits a given labour force to produce. But output is composed of consumption goods and investment goods. To compare techniques, we must specify how the output is made up. The simplest basis for the comparison is to postulate that it applies to economies that are all growing at the same rate. Each one, that is to say, is carrying out investment in such a way as to keep its stock of capital goods, whatever they may be, increasing at the same proportional rate as all the rest. Each stock of capital goods is of a composition and age structure appropriate to its own equilibrium position and to the rate of growth.

Now compare two economies, Aleph and Beth, each in equilibrium with normal prices ruling in all markets, with equal labour forces, fully employed, both growing at the same rate. Money-wage rates are the same in both. All wage incomes are consumed. In Aleph a smaller proportion of profit income is consumed than in Beth (s_p is greater in Aleph). The rate of profit on capital is consequently lower in Aleph. Money prices are lower and the real-wage rate higher. Each economy is using the technique[1] that yields the highest rate of profit, given its own level of costs and prices (which are confidently expected to remain constant in the future). Since each economy has access to the other's blue-prints, it follows that the Beta technique, in use in Beth, would yield a lower rate of profit at Aleph prices than the Alpha technique which is in use there. And conversely.

In a loose general sense, we may say that the Alpha technique (chosen where the real-wage rate is higher and the rate of profit lower) is more 'capital intensive' than the Beta technique (apart from certain cranky cases which we need not discuss[2]). Output per head is, generally, higher in each line of production taken separately. Where there is some choice as to the time-

---

[1] A technique comprises the whole inter-related complex of production. It corresponds to Sraffa's 'system'.

[2] Cf. my *Accumulation of Capital*, p. 109.

pattern of production, gestation periods for the construction of plant may be longer and there may be a longer recoupment period for the recovery of the value of fixed investment. In a crude sense more, or more elaborate, equipment is required. But the difference cannot be expressed in any simple way as a difference in the ratio of 'capital' to labour. The items entering into different techniques are physically different, so that a direct comparison of the stocks of capital goods, in terms, say, of tons of steel[1] per man, or horse-power per man, is at best very rough. Moreover, since not only the general level, but also the pattern of prices is different when the rate of profit is different, we cannot compare the stocks of capital in terms of their values in any meaningful way.

To overcome this difficulty, we evaluate the two stocks of capital goods at a single rate of profit. Imagine that, while everything remains the same in physical terms, prices are notionally adjusted so that the rate of profit is reduced in Beth and raised in Aleph. In Aleph, as the real-wage rate falls, the advantage in profitability of Alpha over Beta technique is reduced. And as the real-wage rate rises in Beth, the advantage of Beta technique is reduced. Somewhere between the two actual rates of profit lies a rate of profit at which the two techniques are equally eligible. On the basis of prices corresponding to that rate of profit we can value the two stocks of capital goods. In Aleph we find that the value of capital on this basis is greater than in Beth. This follows from the general principles of choice of technique. Any given output is produced at the minimum possible cost. The Alpha technique was chosen at a lower rate of profit than that at which the comparison is being made and the Beta technique at a higher rate of profit. Alpha technique is therefore more capital-using and less labour-using, wherever a choice is possible, than Beta technique.[2]

We now compare the physical flows of output of consumer goods in the two economies. It is not immediately obvious

---

[1] Steel, that is, in the common meaning of the word, not in the mysterious sense sometimes given to it which is synonymous with 'capital'.

[2] It is important to observe that the lower actual rate of profit in Aleph is not due, in a causal sense, to having more 'capital' with a lower 'marginal product'. The lower rate of profit is due to having a more thrifty population (I/K is equal to that in Beth and s_p larger). The greater quantity of capital

which is higher. In Aleph the workers consume more than in Beth; consumption by rentier households per unit of capital is less, but the value of the stock of capital may be greater. To look at the problem in another way, a worker producing consumer goods in Aleph has more mechanised equipment to operate and a higher physical output, but the new entry to the labour force is being equipped to the same high level, so that a larger part of the labour force is occupied with investment. Aleph enjoys the advantage of having more capital (in the loose sense) and at the same time carries the burden of greater annual investment to maintain the same proportionate rate of growth.

To find where the balance of advantage lies, we compare Beta and Alpha techniques on the basis of the set of prices at which they yield the same rate of profit. At the notional prices, the real-wage rate is the same in the two economies. The value of capital per man is higher in Aleph and the value of output per man is just sufficiently higher to provide for profit at the notional rate on the additional capital. With Alpha technique, the value of capital, the average value of total annual net output and the annual value of net investment are then all higher than with Beta technique. The excess of value of output bears a relation to the excess of the value of capital given by the notional rate of profit. The excess of value of investment bears a relation to the excess value of capital given by the rate of accumulation.

It follows, that so long as the rate of profit on capital at which the calculation is made exceeds the rate of accumulation, the physical output of consumption goods is higher in Aleph than in Beth.

K_a and K_b are the values of the stocks of capital.

I_a and I_b are the annual net investments.

in Aleph (as reckoned above) is due to the postulate that each economy has the stock of capital goods that is appropriate, in equilibrium, to its own rate of profit.

Although Aleph has a higher value of capital when calculated on the basis of a common rate of profit, the actual value of its capital, at its own rate of profit, may well be less. The actual rate of profit in Aleph is lower than that at which the calculation is made, so that prices of identical products are likely to be lower in Aleph than in Beth. (It must be borne in mind that we calculate all values on the basis of a common rate of money wages.) Cf. p. 92 above.

$Y_a \equiv (I_a + C_a)$ and $Y_b \equiv (I_b + C_b)$ are the annual net outputs, each consisting of the physical goods actually produced, valued at the notional prices.

r is the notional rate of profit.

g is the rate of growth.

$$\frac{Y_a - Y_b}{K_a - K_b} = r \qquad \frac{I_b}{K_b} \equiv g \equiv \frac{I_a}{K_a}$$

$$r > g$$
$$\therefore (Y_a - I_a) > (Y_b - I_b)$$
$$\therefore C_a > C_b.$$

Dividing by the notional prices, the physical output of consumption goods corresponding to C_a is greater than that corresponding to C_b.

Alpha technique has a higher *degree of mechanisation* in the sense that it makes it possible for a given labour force to maintain a higher rate of output of consumption goods than Beta, while maintaining the same proportionate rate of growth.

Ranging the techniques from the given set of books of blueprints in order of the degree of mechanisation on this basis, that with the highest real-wage rate has the highest degree of mechanisation and the highest total consumption per annum for a given number of workers employed.

Thrift and Mechanisation

The highest real-wage rate that can be paid (when there is no saving out of wages) is that which corresponds to the situation where there is no consumption out of profits. It is this wage rate that is compatible with the technique that permits the highest possible level of total consumption to be maintained.[1] When there is no saving out of wages and no consumption out of profits, the rate of profit on capital is equal to the rate of growth of the stock of capital. This is the first part of the theorem which we set out to establish.

---

[1] If workers begin to save, when there is no consumption out of profits, the rate of profit is depressed below the rate of growth. If the technique appropriate to that rate of profit were installed it could be maintained only by keeping consumption below the maximum possible. Mr Luigi Pasinetti has pointed out that if the workers already own a proportion of the stock of capital equal to the ratio of their savings to net investment, the rate of profit is independent of their saving.

Zero Accumulation

When the proposition is put forward in terms of a comparison of stationary states, it appears quite familiar.

Equilibrium in a stationary state requires that the thriftiness conditions should be such that there is some pattern of prices and incomes — that is to say, some rate of profit — at which there is zero net saving. The stock of capital appropriate to that rate of profit is such that the marginal product of investment (the additional output to be obtained by having a little more capital, valued at constant prices) is equal to that rate of profit. (If the degree of mechanisation were lower, and the rate of profit greater, equilibrium would require investment to be going on ; the conditions for a stationary state would not be satisfied.)

Now, if thriftiness conditions are such that saving would occur at any rate of profit greater than zero, stationary equilibrium entails a zero rate of profit. It therefore entails a zero marginal product of investment; that is to say, it requires the largest stock of capital per head that it is of any use to have. The highest possible rate of consumption is then being enjoyed. Since there is no net profit income, there is no consumption out of profits. Gross profits are just sufficient to provide the gross investment which is keeping the stock of capital intact. This is the special case of our proposition which applies when the rate of growth is zero. It corresponds to the state of economic Bliss.

TECHNICAL PROGRESS AND OBSOLESCENCE

To apply the same type of argument to the case of technical progress, we once more set up our question in an artificial way. We now compare economies each with a constant labour force ; as before, full employment obtains, and the money-wage rate is constant. There is a steady rate of autonomous neutral technical progress which is the same for all economies. In the manner described above,[1] we postulate that each economy is divided in a clear-cut manner into an investment sector and a

---

[1] *A Model of Technical Progress*, p. 88 *et seq.*

consumption-good sector ; progress is concentrated on the design of consumption-sector plant. In each economy's investment sector a team of workers, while keeping its own equipment intact, produces equipment for use in the consumption-good sector. Each year they produce a different type of equipment which will yield a higher rate of output per man employed in producing consumption goods compared to the type produced the year before. The increase in productivity is at a constant proportional rate from year to year. Once built, there is no physical change in a batch of equipment ; it has a long potential life and will be discarded only as a result of obsolescence. Competition causes prices to fall with costs (the money-wage rate being constant). A plant is scrapped when the value of its output (net of other inputs) is only just sufficient to pay the wage bill for the workers operating it[1] so that it yields no gross profit. Those workers are then provided with new equipment of the latest design.

Once more, we compare two economies, Aleph, where the real-wage rate is higher, with Beth, where it is lower. The labour force is the same in the two economies. They have passed through the same history of technical development and the latest, most productive, type of plant that has just been installed is of identical design in each. Aleph, where the real wage is higher, has already knocked out some types of plant that are still being used in Beth. The longer tail of older-fashioned plants in Beth reduces the average productivity of its consumption-sector labour. On the other hand, a given plant lives longer in Beth, replacements are less frequent and the proportion of the labour force in the investment sector is less. As before, there is a balance to be struck between the benefit of a higher output per head of consumption-sector workers and the cost of the extra investment that makes it possible.

Imagine, that while everything remains the same in physical terms, the real-wage rate in each economy is notionally set at a level equal to the product per head of workers operating the type of plant which has the average productivity of the consumption-good sector in Beth. (Since progress is exponential,

---

[1] Abstracting from interest on working capital, and assuming no scrap value for discarded plant.

the plant in question is somewhat younger than the average age of those operating in Beth.)

To pay this wage only to the consumption-sector workers would exhaust the whole output of consumption goods actually being produced in Beth. There would be no gross profit on the consumption-good sector to pay the wages of investment workers and provide for rentier consumption. In Aleph, the type of plant in question may be no longer in use. The real-wage rate there is already above the notional level. If the plant is still in use, the notional wage rate is higher than that being paid in Aleph. But it would still leave Aleph with some gross profit, for the productivity of the average plant in Aleph is higher (being of later design) than that of the type selected for the notional experiment. It follows that the output of consumption goods in Aleph is higher than in Beth.[1]

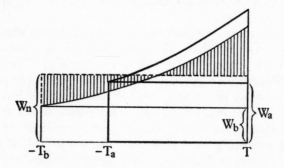

The T represents 'today'. $-T_b$ is the date at which the oldest plant now extant in Beth was new. $-T_a$ is the date at which the oldest plant now extant in Aleph was new. The thick lines refer to Aleph and the fine to lines to Beth. The area enclosed by each represents the respective total rates of output of consumption goods 'today'. The verticals at T represent output of the two batches of plants just installed. That for Aleph is higher, as more men are employed there on each generation of plant, because fewer generations are in use. Similarly, the vertical heights at each point represents the

---

[1] A similar demonstration could have been used in the case of Alpha and Beta techniques. At the real-wage rate at which Beta yields no net profit, Alpha still gives some profit.

outputs of the plants that were new at the corresponding date. W_b is the product of the oldest plant in Beth and is equal to the wage bill for the workers operating each batch. Similarly W_a in Alph. W_n corresponds to the notional real wage. The two shaded areas are equal.

Thrift and Obsolescence

Once more we find that the economy with the highest real-wage rate has the highest level of consumption at each phase of development. The highest wage that can be paid (when workers do not save) is that which obtains when there is no consumption out of profits. The whole of the gross profit on the consumption-good sector is then absorbed by the wages of the investment-sector workers.

In this part of the argument we have avoided referring to the rate of profit on capital, since in connection with technical progress it involves some terminological puzzles.[1] However, when we reckon annual net profit as the rise, over a year, in the value of the stock of capital, reckoned in terms of consumption goods, plus consumption by capitalists, there is no difficulty. In the kind of golden age conditions postulated, with neutral technical progress, the division of the labour force between the sectors, in any one economy, remains constant through time. The money value of the stock of capital remains constant, and the value in terms of consumption goods rises *pari passu* with the real-wage rate, that is, with the rate of growth of output. Thus, when there is no consumption by capitalists, the rate of profit on capital is equal to the rate of growth of the value of the stock of capital.

Our theorem then holds good. When the rate of profit is equal to the rate of growth, the length of life of plant selected is that which yields the maximum level of consumption that can be maintained while growing at a steady rate.

SOCIAL PRODUCT

The inwardness of our theorem can best be seen if we think in terms of a benevolent authority, with complete power over

[1] Cf. above, p. 97.

an economy, who, without paying any attention to the division of product between wages and profits and without discounting the future, is concerned to achieve the highest maintainable rate of growth of consumption.

It is important to distinguish between the once-for-all saving necessary to increase the scale of gross investment relatively to consumption and the continuing abstinence (abstinence, that is, from robbing the future) which is represented by maintaining a given proportion of gross investment. In the present context we are not concerned with the pace or pattern of the once-for-all saving required to reach a desired position, but with a discussion of the desired position itself. Thus, in the case of stationary conditions (a constant labour force and no technical progress or degeneration), the aim of the benevolent planner is Bliss, the situation in which the maximum physically possible permanent level of consumption is being enjoyed and further net saving is otiose. Here we are interested in discussing the position aimed at, first, when the labour force is increasing at a regular autonomous rate and, second, when autonomous neutral technical progress is going on at a steady rate. The planner has no jurisdiction over these growth rates, which he has to take as given by God and the engineers.

From the point of view of the benevolent planner, the product of the widening investment that takes place when new workers are provided with capital goods is the output that they will produce, which they could not have produced if they had not been provided with equipment and jobs. Valuing the cost of the investment and the future flow of product in terms of consumption goods, the marginal efficiency of this investment is the growth rate of the economy. Deepening investment, which takes the form of providing a group of workers with equipment for a more mechanised technique than that which they have been operating, has a social product which consists in the additional flow of output that they will now produce. The concepts of deepening and widening do not apply in general to the case of technical progress. Our highly formalised type of neutral progress can, however, be treated in these terms. The gross investment that maintains a rate of growth of output equal to the rate of growth of output per head is a kind of widening. To speed up obsolescence in such a way as to raise output at a given stage of technical development is a kind of deepening.

The process of deepening (in either sense) requires once-for-all saving. We are here concerned, not with the process of once-for-all saving, but with the stage to which the deepening process will be carried. If the authority sees that deepening would increase the permanently maintainable rate of growth of consumption,[1] he has it carried out. We are not going into the question of how long it will take or how he organises the requisite once-for-all saving.

Our benevolent authority pushes deepening to the point where the marginal efficiency of deepening investment is equal to the marginal efficiency of widening; that is, till it is equal to the growth rate of the economy. There is then nothing to be gained by deflecting any further resources from producing for current consumption to gross investment.

In our private-enterprise economies, the firms were not choosing to grow at the growth rate. We simply postulated that each economy was growing in such a way as to maintain full employment. No individual in the private-enterprise economy need be supposed to be conscious of what the overall growth rate is. They *are* conceived to be making conscious choices about the techniques selected from the book of blue-prints. When a firm finds itself in such a situation that, at current prices, the return on a sum of money invested in Alpha plant would be a shade less than in Beta, it does not invest in Alpha. The stage which deepening reaches is held up at the point where its marginal product to the individual firm is equal to the rate of profit on capital. When the rate of profit on capital exceeds the rate of growth (that is, when there is consumption out of profits) the private-enterprise firms are

---

[1] Where the choice of technique involves the time-pattern of investment (for instance, longer-lived plant gives a greater total output spread over a longer future at a lower rate per annum), he makes his calculation by discounting the future flow of output at a rate of interest equal to the growth rate of the economy (which is autonomously given by the rate of growth of the labour force and the flow of improvements in the design of plant). This is not because our planner discounts the future, but because present output has a physical, technical superiority over future output in the sense that it can potentially be reinvested and made to grow at the growth rate.

refraining from undertaking deepening investment that the benevolent authority would undertake. Similarly, an individual firm does not scrap plant that is yielding some gross profit,[1] whereas the benevolent authority is guided not by profit but by the increment in total output per head that could be achieved with improved plant. When there is consumption out of profits, so that the real wage is lower than that which corresponds to the optimum length of life of plant, replacements are not being made that the benevolent authority would undertake.

The behaviour of the firms and of the benevolent authority coincide only when the rate of profit on capital is equal to the rate of growth of the economy.

CONCLUSION

It is not legitimate to draw practical conclusions, without further consideration, from an argument, such as the above, which is concerned only with the logical implications of a postulated state of equilibrium. In particular, it must be remarked that under private enterprise a *rise* in thriftiness is more likely to produce a slump than an improvement in the selection of technique and that it is more onerous to provide for an *increase* in the degree of mechanisation or a *speeding up* of obsolescence than to maintain a higher level that has already been attained. Nevertheless, if there is any rough correspondence between reality and the type of analysis here set out, the fact that the rate of profit on capital may be of the order of 15 or 20 per cent in an economy that is growing at the rate of 2 or 3 per cent per annum, does suggest some interesting lines of thought.

APPENDIX

(1) *The Wicksell Process*

There has been a recent revival of interest in Wicksell's problem of a process of deepening investment (with a constant

---

[1] We are abstracting from interest on working capital and various other considerations that may cause earlier scrapping in reality.

Appendix

labour force and a set of blue-prints of known techniques given once and for all) carried out in neo-classical equilibrium so that the profit-maximising marginal productivity conditions are continuously fulfilled.[1]

There are two major difficulties in this analysis. The first concerns the question of foresight. As the process goes on, the rate of profit falls. Are the entrepreneurs aware that this will happen, and if so, how are they to make the correct selection of types of long-lived plant to ensure that profit-maximising techniques are always in use?

One way to evade the difficulty is to postulate that the process goes on very slowly and plant is relatively short-lived, so that even though firms act on the assumption that the present rate of profit will continue to obtain in the future, the errors in investment planning are not serious. (This is rather in the nature of the housemaid's excuse.) Another is to postulate that all capital goods are made from a homogeneous, indestructible material called *steel* or *Meccano*, which might better be named *ectoplasm*. It can be shifted from one use to another and moulded into different forms without cost, so that there can never be any mistaken investments. In this case no foresight is needed.[2]

I prefer to go the whole neo-classical hog and assume correct foresight. Then the expected fall in the rate of profit on investment expresses itself in a spectrum of interest rates for loans of different terminal dates, which guides the firms in making investments in plants of various expected future working lives.

The second difficulty concerns the motive for accumulation.

[1] See my 'Accumulation and the Production Function', *Economic Journal*, September 1959, and *Collected Economic Papers*, Vol. ii, for a number of recent discussions of this problem. Since then an elaborate treatment has been offered by Professor Meade — *A Neo-Classical Theory of Economic Growth*. Meade allows for steady growth with an increasing labour force and technical progress, as well as pure deepening.

[2] In the case where ectoplasm per man employed is always larger in the ectoplasm-producing sector of the economy than in the consumption-good sector, ectoplasm will become redundant and its price sink to zero at some point in the process of decelerating accumulation. If ectoplasm is not indestructible, a process of decumulation (not accumulation) can take place under equilibrium conditions. The story starts with an indefinitely large stock of ectoplasm and runs down to the stationary state from above. This was pointed out to me by Dr. H. Uzawa.

How is it that full employment is maintained in face of a continually falling rate of profit ? Sometimes a fixed ratio of saving to income is postulated (the *s* of Harrod's formula), the marginal productivity conditions being relied upon to determine the ratio of income to capital. Sometimes a Keynesian element is introduced ; the proportion of saving in profits is allowed to be greater than in wages, while marginal productivity is relied upon to determine the distribution of income. The rate of interest is then said to be adjusted in such a way as to make net investment equal to the rate of saving at each moment of time.

This seems to lead into confusion. Given the labour force (which must always be fully employed), the book of blue-prints of known techniques and the propensities to consume (whether Harrodian or Keynesian), there is a fully specified path that the economy must follow. At each point on it the past is entailed just as much as the future is determined. (In logical time, unlike historical time, there is no rule of one-way traffic.) At each point the marginal productivities are determined and the rate of interest has to be in equilibrium with them. It cannot also be used to jolly the investors along to fulfil their pre-destinate fate.[1]

Once more, it seems to me better to go the whole hog and simply postulate that accumulation is such as to maintain full employment under equilibrium conditions. The propensities to save then come into the story as one of the determinants of the shape of the equilibrium path. For instance, if thriftiness conditions are of the Harrod type, expressed by the overall ratio of saving to income, *s*, an economy with a higher value of *s* has a lower ratio of consumption to net investment at each point on its path, compared to one with a lower *s*. If the thriftiness conditions are of a Keynesian type, an economy where a higher proportion of profits is consumed has a lower real-wage rate and a less mechanised technique than another (with more thrifty capitalists) has at each corresponding point on *its* path.

---

[1] It is quite another matter to deploy a story in historical time, not logical time, in which, starting from some arbitrary position, the authorities arrange for investment that will absorb full-employment saving from then on. In such a story the marginal-productivity conditions will not normally be fulfilled, though at each moment firms may be planning to fulfil them in the future. Cf. above, p. 58.

Appendix

All this concerns the equilibrium path with some arbitrarily given thriftiness conditions. There is quite another question, which is : At what rate ought deepening investment to be carried out ? In terms of our benevolent planner, when he has fixed on the degree of mechanisation that will be in use at Bliss, how fast should he set about building up the stock of capital goods that will be required when he gets there ?

This was the original theme of Frank Ramsey's famous article. It seems to be impossible to find an answer, within the framework of neo-classical analysis, unless we are provided with a calculus for evaluating the utilities of different individuals, at different dates, as well as with a satisfactory answer to the old complaint : What did posterity ever do for us ?

The problem, however, is one which comes up in real life. In actual societies thriftiness conditions are not just given, as they are in a journal article. They are affected by the distribution of wealth within each class, as well as between classes; they are influenced by taxation, by advertising, credit arrangements and all the rest of it. Once we begin to think in terms of welfare as a real-life subject (instead of as a branch of pure mathematics) we have to take a view as to what rate of accumulation is desirable ; when the rate of accumulation has been decided upon (on whatever principles), thriftiness has to be moulded (either way) so that it can take place without unemployment or inflationary pressure.

This is a very large part of the problem for underdeveloped economies which are seeking to industrialise. It has some application also nearer home.

(2) History of the Theorem

As this theorem seems to have aroused some interest, I give its history so far as I know it. The proposition that, in the absence of technical progress, consumption per man employed is at the maximum when all profits are saved and all wages spent follows immediately when we combine a Keynesian theory of profits with a properly articulated neo-classical production function. It is implicit in the comparison of golden ages with the same rate of growth and different thriftiness conditions (discussed, for instance, by Professor R. F. Kahn in 'Exercises in the Analysis of Growth', *Oxford Economic Papers*, June 1959, p. 148), but I first saw it explicitly stated by Professor Swan, in terms of the marginal product of 'capital', in the draft of his paper for the International Economic Association meeting at Gamagori in 1960.

It has been made the basis for a satirical sketch set in the country of Solovia by Professor Phelps ('The Golden Rule of Accumulation', *American Economic Review*, September 1961), which appeared after the foregoing essay had been written.

I came across the application of the proposition to the optimum length of life plant some years ago in the course of an argument with Mr. Eltis and Dr. Garegnani who were then attending my lectures. Professor Champernowne backed me up with a neat mathematical proof. Another pupil, Mr Pai Panandikar, wrote it up in a complicated form which I do not think was ever published. I did not find the above simple proof until I was writing this essay.

When we think of the proposition in terms of the condition that the workers consume the whole wage and capitalists save the whole profit, it appears somewhat mysterious. When we realise that it does not matter at all who does the saving so long as the rate of profit is equal to the rate of growth, it seems fairly obvious.

INDEX

THE END